God's Speaking

R.E. Clark

GnG Publishers
122 Skinner St.
Centerton, AR 72719

First Edition
Published by GnG Publishers
3/31/2015

Printed in the United States of America
Cover photo and back cutout courtesy: Gordon Adler
Dipl.Designer (FH)
Dorfstrasse 23
39599 Käthen
GERMANY

ISBN-13: 978-0692406083
ISBN-10: 0692406085

DEDICATION

To the faithful believers who have shown me through many
years of ministry that God is always pleased by a life of
faith.

Table of Contents

ACKNOWLEDGMENTS

When I began to write my first book a few years back, I assumed it would be not only my first, but my last. It was not because I lacked joy in the process. I just assumed that the few copies awarded to the author would be all I would ever see in print. I was so wrong! God has blessed me immensely through so many who have read and are still reading the words He has given me. I am also blessed by the pleasure of writing these words upon pages that have become not one, but several books.

As a boy I always had a desire to be an artist. So much so, that I asked for a set of pastel chalks as a Christmas gift. I imagined myself becoming a landscape artist that would paint canvases of beautiful sunsets. Many of you have responded to my writing with words of encouragement. You have enlightened me to the understanding that I can paint with words. I thank you for your kindness. By the way, I never did use that chalk set to its full potential!

My daughter, Kayre Chastain, has once again served as my proofreader and forthright editor. I always appreciate her willingness to serve in this capacity and to offer suggestions that help me to better capture just the right words. Sometimes words are much like one of those sunsets that I wanted to paint as a boy. They appear for a brief moment and then they are gone forever.

I could not complete any book without the loving support of my wife, Trudy. Lovingly, she allows me the time to seize those special moments in time and "paint" my thoughts for you to read and use in your Christian walk.

.

PREFACE

God speaking…

The world seems to always have at least one and often times many who appear on the scene with a word from God. Of course, the response that is most often heard when someone declares that they are speaking for God follows these lines, "They're crazy!"

This book is not about me delivering a word from or even for God. My intent in writing *God's Speaking,* is to help you understand that God *really* is speaking today. He is speaking in the same way today as He declared through the writer of Hebrews—through His Son, Jesus.

> "God, who at various times and in various ways spoke in time past to the fathers by the prophets, has in these last days spoken to us by His Son, whom He has appointed heir of all things, through whom also He made the worlds;" (Hebrews 1:1-2)

Over the years of my preaching ministry I began to use Hebrews 11 for a series of messages on the subject of faith. This one chapter is noted by many as the "Faith Chapter" or as "God's Hall of Faith." I began to discover, as I studied and preached through this one chapter, God's intent in including these particular characters in this faith list. To be honest, some did not appear to pull off the faith life with great success.

What then was the message of Hebrews 11? It was none other than *God's Speaking*! Clearly, God saw fit that the lives of these particular people would be used like loud speakers from heaven to declare His own voice. In each life, though frail and failing, God was clearly speaking.

It is my hope as you read this book that you will hear God speaking to you. Not only is it my desire that you hear God speak, but that you enter this experience with one purpose: To Obey!

As I have preached and taught this message multiple times across the country, I have engaged the congregations to rehearse these words again and again: **God Speak—I Obey!** I pray that you will whisper those words as you begin this journey with me. Make it your intent to obey for I truly believe that God is speaking!

Chapter One

THE SUBSTANCE OF FAITH

Hebrews chapter 11 is a great place to delve into the subject of faith. The entire chapter is a list of one person after another that engaged a life of faith. While I will lay certain foundational truths before you, I will also keep referring again and again to the fact that God is using the lives of those listed in His Hall of Faith to speak.

The assertion I want to make is not that God has spoken, but that He *is* speaking. We have only to obey.

Interestingly, obedience not only is the response to His speaking, but it is the opening of our spiritual ears to hear Him speaking in the first place. In other words, you must have an attitude to obey before He speaks, so that as He is speaking we can obey. All of this requires faith at work in our lives. We obey without knowing the command to which we have agreed to act upon in obedience. You will never do this without the energizing of faith.

A full and clear understanding of faith is a prerequisite to this process. This is why the writer of Hebrews by the inspiration of the Holy Spirit expresses a solid definition of faith before he commences to give the life examples that encompass the remainder of Hebrews chapter 11.

This might be a good time to let you know who the writer of Hebrews is. Honestly, no one knows for sure and it does not really carry any significance in this particular study. Some believe that it is none other than the Apostle Paul himself. The King James Version of the Bible titles this book, "The Epistle of Paul the Apostle to the Hebrews." I believe that to be the case, though I will not go to task with anyone who believes differently. I will, however, from this point on refer to Paul as the writer. You are free to insert another name or the generic format of the writer. At the minimum, we will agree that the book is the inspired word of God.

FAITH'S DEFINITION

Since it is God's inspired and infallible word, we can gain real assurance from the definition given for faith in the opening of the eleventh chapter.

Now faith is the substance of things hoped for, the evidence of things not seen. (Hebrews 11:1)

These first few words settle the fact that faith is much more that a holy hope so. For many faith is nothing more than just that: a sanctified hope bathed in religious terminology that is based on nothing more than a whimsical wish. There is an element of hope involved, but it has substance upon which it rests.

Faith is not the result of our hope, but our hope rests upon and is made sure by the fact that faith stands under

2

what we are hoping for in any given circumstance. Faith gives us the title deed to our hope even if we do not yet hold that which we have hoped for at the moment. So Paul asserts that faith is the evidence of things not seen.

Now before you think that the whole business of faith is merely some mystical fantasy, you must realize that faith has a basis for its existence. Faith cannot exist in isolation. It cannot be unless it has an object upon which to rest and a subject upon which its force might reside.

Simon Kistemaker, who co-authored the *Baker New Testament Commentary: Hebrews*, asserts the following: "faith is adhering to the promises of God, depending on the Word of God, and remaining faithful to the Son of God." In this three part description of faith's foundation you can see both the basis for faith's existence and the necessity of our part in the equation.

Faith is loyal to and rests upon the promises of God. It is not conjecture or some contrivance of religious activity. Faith can exist because God has spoken. Faith can be a viable part of our everyday lives because God *is* speaking. Faith is the result of trusting what God has promised because we know by faith through the word of God that He cannot lie.

Paul stated it clearly as he wrote to Titus, "Paul, a bondservant of God and an apostle of Jesus Christ, according to the faith of God's elect and the acknowledgment of the truth which accords with godliness, in hope of eternal life which *God, who cannot lie*, promised before time began," (Titus 1:1-2 *emphasis mine*).

I suppose there is no greater example of resting upon the promise of God than can be found in the life of Abraham. This Old Testament patriarch trusted God's promise to get to the land of which he knew nothing, and of even greater evidence he believed God when it came to his own progeny. Abraham waited upon God and saw the promise of God fulfilled in the miracle of Isaac's birth.

Paul speaks of Abraham's faith in the spoken promises of God in several of his writings. In Romans Paul declares that Abraham believed God and it was accounted unto him for righteousness (Romans 4:20-22). In the book which we have here under consideration, Paul once again falls back upon the faith actions of Abraham. But in this instance Paul lays firmly the basis for faith upon God himself and not upon the frailty of man—even a man of faith like Abraham.

"For when God made a promise to Abraham, because He could swear by no one greater, He swore by Himself, saying, 'Surely blessing I will bless you, and multiplying I will multiply you.' And so, after he had patiently endured, he obtained the promise. For men indeed swear by the greater, and an oath for confirmation is for them an end of all dispute. Thus God, determining to show more abundantly to the heirs of promise the immutability of His counsel, confirmed it by an oath, that by two immutable things, in which it is impossible for God to lie, we might have strong consolation, who have fled for refuge to lay hold of the hope set before us." (Hebrews 6:13-18)

Here again we see that God cannot lie because it is impossible for Him to do so. Faith then exists in the adherence to God's unfailing promise; a promise that is fixed upon God's own oath to fulfill what He has agreed to in covenant. This truth helps us to trust that which is unseen.

In Genesis 15 God commanded Abraham to take several animals: a three year old heifer, a three year old female goat, a three year old ram, a turtledove, and a pigeon. He was to divide these in half and lay the pieces of the animal carcasses along each side of a pathway created by their severed bodies. This scene would have been familiar to Abraham. In his day two individuals would do all of this in preparation for a covenant between them both.

After dividing the animals the two would walk hand and hand along the pathway lined with the bodies of the animals. After passing through and out of the path, they would then make covenant and declare that the same death would befall either of them who failed to keep his part of the bargain.

Interestingly, God caused a deep sleep to fall upon Abraham and God appeared in a vision as a smoking oven and a burning torch. God then passed along through the animal carcass pathway as He demonstrated exactly what you just read above in the verses from Hebrews 6.

God swore allegiance to His own promises by His own presence because there was no greater by which to swear by. He knew that Abraham's faith would fail, but that His own word could not. God spoke—Abraham obeyed and the rest as they say is history.

Faith then is loyalty to the promises of God as revealed in the word of God. It is the word of God as spoken to the prophets of old that we can still depend upon today. This is the guarantee and the validation of that which we hear God speaking in this day.

God cannot nor will He speak anything that is contrary to His written word. The Bible becomes the litmus test for all that God speaks. We have the responsibility to test what we hear by what God has already spoken in His word.

In this day when "God hearers" are coming out of the woodwork, we have reassurance that God speaks only that which can be corroborated by what He has seen fit to have recorded in the Bible. Herein, is the importance of our belief in an infallible, inerrant, and inspired scripture. Without this foundational truth we have no way to know for sure what we are hearing God speak. This is especially true when someone says to you, "God told me..."

Kistemaker concluded his three part definition with this: "faith is...remaining faithful to the Son of God." As stated in the preface of this book: This book is not about me delivering a word from or even for God. My intent in writing *God's Speaking,* is to help you understand that God *really* is speaking today. He is speaking in the same way today as He declared through the writer of Hebrews—through His Son, Jesus.

> "God, who at various times and in various ways spoke in time past to the fathers by the prophets, has in these last days *spoken to us by His Son*, whom He has appointed heir of all things, through whom also He made the worlds;" (Hebrews 1:1-2, *emphasis mine*)

It was Jesus who declared throughout His entire earthly ministry that He spoke only that which had been given to Him by His Father. When those in authority asked Jesus who He was, he responded, "I have many things to say and to judge concerning you, but He who sent Me is true; and I speak to the world those things which I heard from Him." (John 8:26) Continuing he said, "...that I do nothing of Myself; but as My Father taught Me, I speak these things..." (John 8:28).

To hear Jesus speaking is to hear God speaking. Again, the words of Jesus testify to this fact. "For I have not spoken on My own authority; but the Father who sent Me gave Me a command, what I should say and what I should speak. And I know that His command is everlasting life. Therefore, whatever I speak, just as the Father has told Me, so I speak." (John 12:49-50)

This is why Paul can so quickly transition from the definition of faith in verse 1 to the immediate results of faith in verse 2. If faith based upon God's speaking directly to us is true, then the natural result will be the testimony of those who have heard.

The elders, our forefathers, and all who have heard before us will give a solid report because of God's speaking. Their lives and deaths will be the testimony of faith at work as they heard God speaking directly to them. Our English translations state that the elders "obtained a good testimony" by faith. This phrase is one word in the original Greek translation. Literally, the verse reads, For by it (faith) the elders became martyrs.

I can hear a collective gasp from you as this fact sinks in on your belief system. In this world of "easy-believism" and soft church pews, it's a little difficult to attach faith to martyrdom. This is especially hard to grasp with an American church mindset.

Faith to many is a system by which we put God in an arm hold until He relents to our wishes. Often faith produces nothing but an unfounded hope in our own cognitive reasoning. We cannot imagine a faith that would lead to trial or tribulation, much less death. The only faith that will result in hearing God speaking is a faith that can carry you all the way through death, including a martyr's death.

Had I written this book just a few years back I probably would have glossed over lightly the idea of martyrdom. But one only has to look just beneath the surface of the nightly news to find story after story of those who are living the ultimate faith life. The ground is soaking in daily the blood of countless thousands who after hearing God speak have freely laid down their lives for the sake of the gospel.

I wrote the following in the second book of this series, *God's Designing.* It is available on Amazon or directly from me:

There are two distinct types of martyrs. You will find evident throughout history both the Christian martyr and the religious martyr.

I use the word Christian here to identify the born-again believer only. I use the word religious in a very broad sense. This person may be martyred for many reasons which may be religious, but particularly, martyrdom occurs as a result of some avid belief. That belief bears ideals that attain to the height of religious fervor and fanaticism.

The distinction in these two is thus noted: Where the religious martyr lives to die, the Christian martyr dies in order to live.

Jimmy Draper speaking of the original meaning of martyrdom said, "The death of Christians did not make them martyrs; it only revealed them to be martyrs. They were martyrs long before they gave up their lives!"

Leighton Ford noted in his book, One Way to Change the World, "What then is a martyr? He is a confessor. A martyr is one who is first convinced of a truth, and then yields his life to the claims of the truth of which he is convinced, and who, therefore, is changed by the truth which he believes, and to which he had yielded himself…A martyr is a specimen, an evidence, a sample, a credential, a proof, a witness."

This is where faith requires us to be true to the Son of God. It is when we are willing to hear His call to "Follow Me" that we begin a wonderful journey of daily living with an anticipation to hear Him speaking. The only way we can take up our cross daily and follow Him is when we hear Him speaking clearly. Sometime, maybe in your life or mine, He may speak to you or I the words that will lead to our own martyrdom. In that moment, there must be a calm assurance that can only be brought to pass by a faith that rests upon God's promises, depends upon God's word, and remains true to God's Son.

FAITH'S KNOWLEDGE

With the matter of faith's definition settled, we should be able to move on, right? Well, not exactly…

Do you remember when you were in grade school? That's a long time back for some, but you will most likely remember this scenario. You asked the teacher how to spell a word and to your dismay she responded, "Look it up!"

Don't you have to know how to spell a word in order to look it up? Perhaps worse than that was when you asked, "What does this word mean?" Again, the teacher gave the same response, "Look it up!" To the dictionary you return at least with the assurance that you know how to spell the word you are seeking to define. However, the definition just left you scratching your head.

This leads you to another couple of questions. "Why don't they put pictures in the dictionary?" "Don't they know that a picture speaks a thousand words?" Well, God must have known about you and me and a few million more believers who would come along needing more than just a simple definition built out of words. Thankfully, God uses pictures!

Not only does God use pictures, He draws them in such a way that no one can miss the truth He wants to reveal. Paul follows the definition and the testimony of faith with these words:

"By faith we understand that the worlds were framed by the word of God, so that the things which are seen were not made of things which are visible." (Hebrews 11:3)

Now that's what I'm talking about! A definition **with** a picture!

Our knowledge of faith is pictured in the creation of the world and framed by the word of God. God makes us understand the definition of faith (something unseen) by looking to something that is readily seen all around us; the world in which we live. God literally created the world so that faith would be produced in each believer.

There are most likely some who will read this and may at this point assume that they can read no further because they cannot wrap their minds around a Creator who created all that is. This same person who cannot accept by faith the fact that God created all that is out of nothing, so that all that is can be accepted by nothing more than faith, will in the same instant believe that all that is came from something that somehow was already there in the vast expanse of time past.

Furthermore, this person who cannot accept a Creator by faith, will by faith (although they will not call it such) believe that this great something collided with another great something and out of the chaotic explosion all that is visible was formed. If this is the case, we should have never rescued the failing auto manufacturers in the first decade of this century. We would have been better served by bombing all of the junk yards in America so all the pieces of something that existed there could fly out randomly into perfectly tuned sports cars for all to enjoy!

You laugh. At least I hope you are laughing. This is only one example of what happens when a person no longer understands faith. That person will always resort to some ludicrous concept that actually takes more faith to believe than the original picture of faith drawn by God.

It is the creation itself that leads us to faith and faith itself leads us to the Creator. Genesis begins with the simple faith statement, "In the beginning God…" Satan knows this to be true. He was a witness to it all unfolding from the very spoken word of God. Do you see it? God began all of this by speaking. He maintains it all by speaking. He will dispense of it all by speaking. ***God is speaking!***

Now you know why the world spends so much time trying to arrest the minds of your children on the subject of the creation. If you start your journey of faith wrong you will never wind up at the right destination. Some may drift from the truth, but the seed of truth is still there and can be used to draw a person back out of error. If, however, I can get you started wrong from the very first step, then I have made the experiment much easier to control.

Life then becomes a series of chance encounters that are explained away by flawed human reason. The world defines

11

seeing as believing; the Christian defines life as believing in order to see.

What a picture God has drawn for us! He declares in Psalm 19:1, "The heavens declare the glory of God; and the firmament shows His handiwork." You don't even have to go to the bookshelf for a dictionary. You never have to know how to spell the word. God will never say, "Go look it up!" He will only say, "Look up and see what I have already laid out as the evidence of faith!"

God needed nothing to work with when He created all that is. He needed nothing to work with when He called you to follow Him. The creation is the evidence and the picture of God's work in us. Just as He spoke in the beginning He speaks into our lives. You have nothing to bring. He has everything you need. It is beyond our comprehension and yet the scripture clearly declares, "By faith we understand..."

FAITH'S WORSHIP

What is the one thing that all of creation has in common? One thing for sure it's not our ancestors! God created all that we see and experience in nature as well as mankind. Each part of creation fills a particular purpose based upon God, the Creator's, intent.

What then do I have in common with an animal, a tree, or even a rock?

Worship!

Everything that is in existence has its existence for the expressed purpose of worshipping the Creator. The Psalms are filled with such commands as, "Let everything that has breath praise the Lord." (Psalm 150:6)

When Jesus was entering Jerusalem in His triumphal parade the leaders were there demanding that the people stop shouting their hosannas. Jesus told them, "I tell you that if these should keep silent, the stones would immediately cry out." (Luke 19:40)

Worship is the natural outflow of a life of faith and this is where Paul takes us immediately after getting the preliminaries of faith established. He introduces us to the first character in a long list of men and women who reside in this Hall of Faith. This person responded to God's speaking by offering to God a sacrifice. His name was Abel.

Abel was the second born son of Adam and Eve. It is interesting that Paul began where he did in his list of the faithful. He did not begin with Adam and Eve. One might assume that they lost their position in this listing because of their moral failure and the fact that they ultimately brought the penalty of sin upon all mankind, but I think not.

Adam and Eve had heard God speak, but it was a direct communication. God walked with them in the garden. He instructed them face to face as it were. The first couple did not have to live by faith for all was sight.

In Romans 8:24 Paul expresses the futility of having faith when you have already seen. Adam and Eve had no need for faith because they were in a state of sinless communion with God. Their children and you and I who live today are required to live a life of faith—not a life of sight. Four times in scripture this concept is repeated, in Habakkuk 2:4; Romans 1:17; Galatians 3:11; and Hebrews 10:38.

"The just shall live by faith"

Abel is listed as the first person to live totally by faith. Though Adam and Eve certainly had to live by faith after the fall they did not begin that way. Cain, their firstborn, rejected faith totally and tried to substitute works in its place even though scripture clearly highlights the fact that he had heard God speaking as to what was required of him.

After he had experienced God rejecting his offering, God said, "Why are you angry? And why has your countenance fallen? If you do well, will you not be accepted? And if you do not do well, sin lies at the door. And its desire is for you, but you should rule over it." (Genesis 4:6-7) Clearly, he knew what was the right thing to do. God had spoken through his parents and through their own sacrificial offerings. It was his disobedience to what God had spoken that brought disaster to his life.

Abel, after hearing God speak, responded in faithful obedience. Paul lets us know without a doubt that Abel's offering was more excellent (Hebrews 11:3) because it was offered in faith. Yes, the spilling of an animal's blood was required, but in essence a lima bean is just as good as a lamb in and of itself. It was faith that made the difference in the offerings of these two brothers.

They had heard the same instruction. They had the same parents. They lived under the same circumstances. They were each other's total sphere of peer pressure. In the end, it was faith that made the difference. God speaks—I obey. Without that, the results are tragic.

When Abel set out to worship God in faith and by faithfully obeying His command, God honored him with righteousness. Just as the elders in Hebrews 11:2 had obtained a testimony, Abel obtained one in the same manner by faith, in Hebrews 11:4. Remember, that the phrase obtained a testimony (11:2) and obtained witness (11:4) are one word in the original Greek text. The word is *martureo*. It is the word from which we derive our English word martyr.

In Abel's case, soon after God testified to his faithfulness he was indeed martyred. His brother being angered at God's rejection of his offering killed Abel. It is interesting that Paul begins the list of the faithful with a martyr. Perhaps there is much more to this business of hearing God speak and deciding to obey His word than we wish to dwell upon in the 21st century church.

Abel could face martyrdom not because he had given his testimony, but because God had testified of him! The world is not so impressed about what you have to say about God, but what God has to say about you!

The life of the believer is inconsequential in the grand scheme of things. Most Christians spend their lives trying to figure out the best way to spend their lives. The example Abel left was written upon his tombstone after a martyr's death:

Through Faith He Being Dead Still Speaks
Hebrews 11:4

What legacy will you leave after the dust of your life settles? Will all you have done be written as the Psalmist said, "For all our days are passed away in thy wrath: we spend our years as a tale that is told." (Psalm 90:9, KJV)

Bob Gass sums up this verse well in his daily devotional book, *A Fresh Word for Today*. He wrote on the matter of the time crunch that we often find ourselves in, "When you die, what will others remember you for—the good times you had or the difference you made? You, and only you, have the power to answer that question." When all of life is done only that which was lived out in faith shall last. God speaks. Obey. And after you have departed this Earth your life will still be speaking.

FAITH'S TRANSFER

I know that it's never going to happen, but I would like to be able to say one day, "Beam me up, Scottie" and expect to dematerialize in one place and pop over to another place in a flash. This may be a sci-fi wish that will never happen, but something very similar happened to the next character in Paul's faith list.

"By faith Enoch was taken away so that he did not see death, 'and was not found, because God had taken him'; for before he was taken he had this testimony, that he pleased God." (Hebrews 11:5)

Enoch got "beamed up." The word that is translated "taken" in this verse literally means to be transferred. It is a change of proximity and a change of position. For Enoch, it all happened by faith as he responded in obedience to God's speaking.

In the case of Abel, we see the justification of faith as he offered the sacrifice of obedience. In Enoch's case, we see the translation of faith. Obedience to God's voice in faith produces radical changes!

As Paul spoke to the church at Colosse, he said, "He {*Jesus*} has delivered us from the power of darkness and conveyed us into the kingdom of the Son of His love, (Colossians 1:13, emphasis mine). The word *conveyed* found in this verse carries the same idea of transferring from one place to another, one realm to another, or in this case, another kingdom.

This is exciting news! We may not have a Scottie standing by at the controls of a transporter on the deck of a spaceship, but we have a Savior who has all the power to change us radically just as Enoch was. Not only changed, but allowed to remain right here as witnesses to His power.

Did you see the word testimony once again in this verse? "Before he was taken, he had this testimony, that he pleased God." From the elders, to Abel, and now to Enoch, each were living the life of a martyr. Remember, you don't die to become a martyr—you die because you already are!

This verse notes the fact that before Enoch was taken he pleased God. What exactly does it mean to please God? Does it mean that we must be a super-saint? Is it even possible to live a life like Enoch in our world today? It takes a better understanding of what the word please means before we simply dismiss the idea of having a relationship like Enoch had with God.

We will need to go back to Genesis to see more completely why Enoch was mentioned here in Hebrews. Enoch was the son of Jared. His father was the second longest living human being that is recorded in the Bible. He lived 962 years. As a matter of fact, Jared saw the birth of his son Enoch and 365 years later received word that Enoch was no more for God had taken him. In the midst of Enoch's "short" life, he also became a father. His son was Methuselah. It is Methuselah's record for age that still reigns today. He lived for 969 years.

As interesting as all of that is, it really does not carry much weight in explaining Enoch being taken by God. What is important in all of this might be found in this one verse: Genesis 5:22. "After he begot Methuselah, Enoch walked with God three hundred years, and had sons and daughters."

Something happened to Enoch at the birth of Methuselah. Actually, it must have happened during the time that Enoch's wife was pregnant with this baby boy for Enoch named his son Methuselah. Some theologians attribute the meaning of the name to the phrase "after him it shall come." The son of Enoch lived until the year of the Flood.

How would it have been possible for Enoch to name his son with prophetic meaning? Simple. He walked with God! He was in complete lock-step agreement with God. This is the meaning of the word translated as walk. It means to walk apace continually. Enoch was in harmony with God and it seems to have begun about the time of Methuselah's birth.

The prophet Amos recorded this statement about walking with such unity. "Can two walk together, unless they are agreed?" (Amos 3:3) This verse speaks of walking as a unit like individuals marching together in complete unison and under the direction of a single voice.

Enoch pleased God because he marched under the direction of God's voice. God was speaking—Enoch was obeying. The result was that Enoch was transferred out of this world. He became so out of step with this world that the only way he could continue walking in unity with God was to leave it.

God beamed him out, but he left behind a legacy that continued all the way through the Deluge that destroyed the world and unto the delivery of a baby in Bethlehem. Luke lists Enoch in the genealogy of Jesus in Luke 3:37.

Chances are you'll not be beamed up any time soon, but you can make a decision today to walk with God every day. May it be said of your life at its end that your testimony was that you pleased God.

FAITH'S PRECIOUSNESS

In *The Lord of the Rings* J.R.R. Tolkien brings to life the character Gollum. Gollum's life unfortunately intersects the rediscovery of the ring of power. Its power overtakes him and he is driven by its possession. The ring becomes for him *His Precious*. He is willing to suffer all to have this ring. For Gollum and others the price of bearing the ring is heavy.

If I may, I would liken faith to this ring of power. As in *The Lord of the Rings*, the entire story unfolds around the effect that his ring has or could have upon each character. Faith is a powerful force. It changes lives, but here is the greater truth:

Without faith you cannot be in agreement with God.

From the previous verse we considered (11:5) Paul concludes the look at Enoch's earthly life with these words, "he had this testimony that he pleased God." Enoch was in complete agreement with God. God set the rules of engagement. God spoke and Enoch obeyed.

At this point we are given what might be considered the "ring of power" as far as faith is concerned. Hebrews 11:6 is the key to understanding all of this chapter and it is the crucial element needed in your life if you are going to walk with God. Remember, two cannot walk together (lock-step) unless they are in agreement.

This verse leaves no wiggle room. It states simply, "But without faith it is impossible to please Him, for he who comes to God must believe that He is, and that He is a rewarder of those who diligently seek Him." (Hebrews 11:6)

I would like to back our way into this verse. In doing so it will be easier to get to the faith part of the equation. The verse is explicit when it comes to the element of faith in our lives. Without faith you go nowhere. You cannot take the first step, much less walk successfully with God in your daily journey.

Paul tells us that the person who comes to God to begin with must do so by believing that He is. You cannot come nor will you make this first step on your own. Belief is energized by faith. Faith has its source in the word of God. "So then faith comes by hearing, and hearing by the word of God." (Romans 10:17) There it is again—God's Speaking, My Obeying!

All that is began with God speaking. God said and it was so. God said and it was so. God said and it was so. Day after day throughout the creation account it was God's speaking and creation responding in obedience. It is no different when it comes to salvation or to our everyday walk with Him. God speaks and we have only one recourse. Obey!

If you take Hebrews 11:6 out of the context of this chapter or out of the context of all God has to say about faith, then pleasing God becomes an impossibility. As we say down South, "It ain't gonna happen!" But here is the good news: God gives us the faith to make that first step and then measures faith to us in proportion to the steps He calls us to make in life.

Listen to Paul's words to the church at Ephesus, "For by grace you have been saved through faith, and that not of yourselves; it is the gift of God, not of works, lest anyone should boast." (Ephesians 2:8-9) We are saved *through* faith. The very first step taken towards salvation is created in faith, but that faith did not originate with you. It was spoken into your life by God Himself. It is a gift. You did not work for it; you didn't even wish it into existence. Remember, some would relegate faith to a holy hope so. However, the faith you received in order to believe came by the word of God.

No more than creation could have spoken itself into existence, God's speaking was necessary for all that is to come out of nothing. When God spoke faith into your life, He began with nothing for you had nothing to offer. If you would have had the tiniest particle of faith to begin with then you would boast about it for eternity. The faith to believe did not come from you, therefore, God gets all the glory in your believing. God speaks—You obey.

So to come to God in the first place requires a belief that He exists. To believe that He exists requires faith. The requirement of faith is fulfilled by God Himself. The results of this is that when we believe that God is, then faith works in our lives. When faith is present then we please God. When we please God then we can walk with Him in agreement.

Don't get the cart before the horse! If you read just the first part of Hebrews 11:6, it could be very easy to just throw in the towel. Give up. Turn your back on the whole process. Walk away justifying your actions with the thought of impossibility. Realize that you can please God by a life of faith. He has made it all possible by the gift of faith at the moment of your salvation and He furthermore makes it possible to please Him by measuring out faith to every believer.

Once again the Apostle Paul speaks to this matter. "For I say, through the grace given to me, to everyone who is among you, not to think of himself more highly than he ought to think, but to think soberly, as God has dealt to each one a measure of faith." (Romans 12:3) God has apportioned to each believer the appropriate measure of faith needed to get the job done that He is requiring of you. This is an incredible thought!

I never have to rely on my own abilities to get the work of God done. I never have to worry about whether I can keep up with God's pace as we walk together. He bestows upon us individually exactly the portion of faith needed!

Consider this. Hebrews 11:6 is written to every believer. That means that you cannot please (walk in agreement with) God without faith. At the same time God is giving to every believer on an individual basis exactly the faith needed to walk with Him in agreement, thereby, pleasing Him. If you are a believer there is no excuse for not pleasing God in your daily walk with Him.

Here's where it gets even more interesting. Because God is the One issuing the faith needed to walk in harmony with Him, there should never be anyone who says, "Look at me!" "If you *really* want to be an exceptional Christian, you should walk at *my* pace!" I have a word for statements like these: **RIDICULOUS!**

It's not about you and me; it's all about Him! God equips each of us individually to walk with Him. He gives us the faith to make the first step towards believing that He is and then He gives us the faith needed to keep pace with Him. This never means that all of us will walk at exactly the same speed. Because God is God, He is not restricted by time or space. He can run with some, jog with others, or in the case of Enoch just walk with him.

As God pours a measure of faith into your life you will begin to sense the steps of God. Then you will be able to join Peter in saying, "For to this you were called, because Christ also suffered for us, leaving us an example, that you should follow His steps…" (1 Peter 2:21) Impossible without faith; unstoppable with faith.

At some point along this journey you are going to ask a question. You may have already considered it, but you have been afraid to voice it out loud. I'll go ahead and ask for us both:

What am I going to get out of all this?

It's a good question, but most of us have been taught that it's not proper to serve God expecting anything in return. After all, heaven should be enough, right?

Well, if you take a look at the last part of Hebrews 11:6 you will discover that God has included reward as part of the life of faith. "He is a rewarder of those who diligently seek Him." Many get the part about believing, but most miss the part about expecting anything in return.

This is not about name it and claim it or even blab it and grab it. This has nothing to do about God owing you and I anything…ever! To understand this concept of God being a rewarder will take a little deeper look in the word itself.

The basis for the word translated rewarder in Hebrews 11:6 comes from two words. The first refers to someone who hires another for a certain position. The second is a word which alludes to the one who hires being just in his recompense to those he has hired. If we take this as a picture of God as a rewarder then it becomes clear that God has no obligation in this matter.

In other words, we must dismiss our concept of reward. It is not us seeing the poster offering a reward for some lost object. Then tearing down the poster and going about the work of finding said object. It is not God paying up after we have delivered. It is totally the opposite!

It is us that are the lost objects. We are diligently seeking a way back to God, but being lost forever, it is God who seeks us.

"As it is written: 'There is none righteous, no, not one; there is none who understands; there is none who seeks after God. They have all turned aside; they have together become unprofitable; there is none who does good, no, not one.'" (Romans 3:10-12)

Incredibly, God in His mercy not only seeks us, finds us, and delivers us, He then rewards us for diligently seeking Him. He recompenses us for the gift of faith that He gave us in the first place! Truly, we are saved by grace through faith and it is not one iota of ourselves. It is all a gift from God!

The mystery of this thing called faith will never be understood on this side of eternity. Though you and I will never have our names listed in this Hall of Faith, we are still included in the reward ceremony that awaits us. We may not be an Abel or an Enoch, but we are seekers hired out by a God who is a debtor to no man. God not only hires when He will, but He pays according to His own schedule.

Jesus told a parable that illuminates this fully in Matthew's gospel. "For the kingdom of heaven is like a landowner who went out early in the morning to hire laborers for his vineyard. Now when he had agreed with the laborers for a denarius a day, he sent them into his vineyard. And he went out about the third hour and saw others standing idle in the marketplace, and said to them, 'You also go into the vineyard, and whatever is right I will give you.' So they went. Again he went out about the sixth and the ninth hour, and did likewise. And about the eleventh hour he went out and found others standing idle, and said to them, 'Why have you been standing here idle all day?' They said to him, 'Because no one hired us.' He said to them, 'You also go into the vineyard, and whatever is right you will receive.'"

"So when evening had come, the owner of the vineyard said to his steward, 'Call the laborers and give them their wages, beginning with the last to the first.' And when those came who were hired about the eleventh hour, they each received a denarius. But when the first came, they supposed that they would receive more; and they likewise received each a denarius. And when they had received it, they complained against the landowner, saying, 'These last men have worked only one hour, and you made them equal to us who have borne the burden and the heat of the day.'"

"But he answered one of them and said, 'Friend, I am doing you no wrong. Did you not agree with me for a denarius? Take what is yours and go your way. I wish to give to this last man the same as to you. Is it not lawful for me to do what I wish with my own things? Or is your eye evil because I am good?' So the last will be first, and the first last. For many are called, but few chosen."

Though I have read this parable many times and made an application that seems most logical concerning the outcome of the workers, I think that it bears a new meaning in light of God being a rewarder of those who diligently seek Him.

Just as in the parable Jesus told of the laborers, none of us sought to be hired. The landowner (God) seeks out the workers and sets the wages for each. It is both the landowners right to set the wage and his just right to pay as he has agreed not based upon the amount of work done, but upon His word. The landowner spoke—the workers obeyed. God speaks—we obey.

It is plain and simple for all to see. God as the rewarder (the one doing the hiring) will pay based on His ability to do so and His faithfulness to His own word of agreement with the one hired or in our case saved. Just as all these men in the parable were hired without résumé or merit, we too are saved by grace through faith. Each man was paid in full according to agreement, just as we will be paid in full.

God is no debtor to any person and to each full recompense shall made. In our lost condition we are eligible for the wages of our sin. Being found in grace, we receive the gift of eternal life.

> "For the wages of sin is death, but the gift of
> God is eternal life in Christ Jesus our Lord."
> (Romans 6:23)

FAITH'S RESPONSE

Seeing for many is believing. You may be one of those people who would never buy a pig in a poke, agree to a land deal on prime real estate you have never seen, or buy a car that you have never test driven—me neither—BUT...

Faith is believing without sight. As already mentioned, if you already have that which is hoped for why do you continue to hope? (Romans 8:24) I have a small plaque that reads:

Faith Is Seeing Light When All The World Around You Is Dark!

Noah may have scratched something similar on the inside of the ark's door after it had been securely shut by the hand of God. This man of faith is introduced in Hebrews 11:7-8, "By faith Noah, being divinely warned of things not yet seen, moved with godly fear, prepared an ark for the saving of his household, by which he condemned the world and became heir of the righteousness which is according to faith."

Is there a proper response when called upon to function in faith? Is it expected of us in the early years of the 21st century to have a faith that is similar to that of Noah? What response can you expect from those around you if you decide to hear God speaking and obey? These are good questions and you most likely have a few hundred more to add to the list.

We are living in a time of sensory overload. We not only expect more information, it is readily available at the touch of a few keys. Responding in faith to the word of God is often delayed, if ever obeyed, until we have gathered all the facts. Noah received a word from God and moved forward. He had no video to explain the step-by-step building of an ark. He could not read the blog posts of other ark builders in his world. He had heard God speaking. His response: obedience.

I am not sure if I have ever received a word from God to do something radical. Radical in the sense that it had never been done before, period. I tend to keep in the back of my mind that Solomon said there is no new thing under the sun. I think I might be using this crutch at times to help me make a decision based on the comforting thought that someone else has gone before me.

Not so with Noah...

This verse tells us that Noah was warned by God of things he had never seen. In the list of the unseen would have been, a boat large enough to house samples of the entire animal kingdom, the total destruction of mankind on planet earth, and RAIN! What is rain?

Noah had never seen it rain, yet he spends the next 120 years of his life as a weather man. Day after day after day he predicts that a deluge is coming. Day after day he gives his forecast and day after day the people around him (save his little family) laughed him to scorn. They had never seen rain either. The difference was faith.

A little geology lesson might be necessary here before moving beyond this subject of rain. To better understand the geological conditions of Noah's day, we need to examine the evidence given in the creation account.

In Genesis 1:7 we are told, "Thus God made the firmament, and divided the waters which were under the firmament from the waters which were above the firmament; and it was so." In causing the dry land to appear, God separated the great bodies of water on the earth and also wrapped the Earth in a canopy of water. This "shield" of water vapor would have created a greenhouse effect over all the earth. This is verified in Genesis 2:6 where scripture informs us that "a mist went up from the earth and watered the whole face of the ground." The earth was not watered by rain falling, but by the evaporation of moisture from the ground each day. You have probably seen something similar to this in the miniature greenhouses that you can set on a window sill.

This process of heating the earth each day and the cooling of the night would have brought forth a daily mist that would have made the earth a huge tropical oasis. Rain was not necessary and was unknown to Noah or to those who watched him faithfully build the ark and give his daily forecast: 100% chance of rain!

Now back to the verse at hand. God spoke to Noah about things he had never seen and Noah moved. Honestly, you will never obey the word God has spoken to you until you move. You do not have the privilege of neutrality in the Christian life. As believers we are called to action. As James reminds us, "Thus also faith by itself, if it does not have works, is dead." (James 2:17)

Noah moved with godly fear. Where our English translation uses four words to describe Noah's response to faith, the original uses only one. The best concept of walking in godly fear is found in the word circumspect. This word is defined as looking around cautiously. It also means to be accurate.

I like to think of the word circumspect as functioning within defined parameters. Think of a pasture where animals are allowed to graze. They are free to roam and eat where they please inside the confines of the fence that surrounds them. The fence is not there as a penalty, but as a protection.

Noah moved when God spoke, but his movement was within the parameters of God's grace. Paul used this idea of circumspection in his letter to the Ephesians. "See then that you walk circumspectly, not as fools but as wise, redeeming the time, because the days are evil." (Ephesians 5:15-16) A circumspect walk is guided by wisdom based upon the revealed word of God. It is a walk of obedience in spite of all circumstance. God speaks—I obey.

Faith releases us to obey God even when we don't have all the facts. Though we may not know the full extent of the parameters, we can be sure that He will not let us go beyond His grace. Faith then serves like the fence in my illustration of the pasture.

Faith moves us to function with accuracy in our obedience. When Noah received the warning of the impending flood (though it would be 120 years in coming) he built an ark. A visit back to the book of Genesis details the accuracy of his work. It was not built haphazardly. It was not constructed after his own design. It was brought into existence by faith as he followed God's blueprint. God spoke—Noah obeyed.

> "And **God said** to Noah, "The end of all flesh has come before Me, for the earth is filled with violence through them; and behold, I will destroy them with the earth. Make yourself an ark of gopherwood; make rooms in the ark, and cover it inside and outside with pitch. And this is how you shall make it: The length of the ark shall be three hundred cubits, its width fifty cubits, and its height thirty cubits. You shall make a window for the ark, and you shall finish it to a cubit from above; and set the door of the ark in its side. You shall make it with lower, second, and third decks." (Genesis 6:13-16, emphasis mine)

Why does it seem that so many have such great difficulty living a life of faith and obedience? Why do we cringe when we think of God speaking to us? Why do we think such thoughts as, "What difference can one person make in the face of a world that seems bound and determined to destroy every design of God's perfect creation?"

We have forgotten the importance of the dearest asset God has entrusted us with in this short journey we call life.

Noah did not. The asset of which I speak is our own families! He obeyed God "*for the saving of his household.*" Now that puts faith and obedience in a whole new light. This could be the impetus for you to listen more intently for the voice of God. The question of what difference can you make is answered when you look into the faces of your own dear family and remark, "When God speaks, I will obey!"

Raymond Brown in *The Message of Hebrews* wrote, "In every generation Christian obedience has powerful evangelistic value. Men and women are not only influenced by what we say to them, but by the way we respond to what God says to us." You are being watched! Yes, the God-haters are watching and they are determined to find fault in your faith life. But they are secondary to your own household.

I think the ark had plenty of room to have accommodated thousands had they responded. In 2 Peter 2:5 the scripture calls Noah a preacher of righteousness. He did not hide God's warning from the world. He faithfully preached as he drove nails. He proclaimed the promise of salvation as he plastered pitch within and without making watertight the very vessel that could save all who would enter in by faith. Noah did not dismiss his responsibility to tell everyone that would listen, but *they* were not his primary focus.

It was his family that kept him sawing, nailing, and pitching. It was his family that kept him walking circumspectly to the command of God. He like Enoch that was mentioned earlier walked with God. Enoch walked into the presence of God; Noah walked into the ark. In both cases, these men were separated from the world by faith.

Enoch begat Methuselah whose name meant "after him it shall come." Methuselah lived 969 years contemplating the meaning of his name. He very likely was alive when the first tree was felled by Noah and his sons. He may have seen this giant ark rising up from the floor of the dry earth. Day by day, he would have remembered the story of his father's exit from this world. Day by day, he probably imagined about this stuff called rain. Day by day, he would have experienced a world that grew constantly worse. Day by day, he would have heard the ridicule hurled at his grandson Noah. And finally the day came when he was no more—then the rain.

God had spoken. Noah had obeyed. Now his family and himself were saved. Eight out of a world of God-haters. All saved because God spoke—Noah obeyed.

What is God saying to you today? It's not a command to build an ark, but it may be that He is calling you to walk circumspectly; to live your life accurately based upon faith. As believers, God has called us to be heirs of salvation. He has portioned to you a measure of faith that will be sufficient for the task He has called you to perform.

It matters not if it is the size of the ark displayed openly for all to see or the quiet, faithful walk of Enoch hidden away until you are no more.

God is still speaking—Obey!

Mileposts

How do faith and obedience interact with each other? Can we really hear God speaking without both in place?

_____

_____

_____

_____

How does hope differ from faith?

_____

_____

_____

_____

What part does the faithfulness of God have in the equation of faith? Name one promise of God that your faith rests upon today.

_____

_____

_____

_____

List the four verses from the Bible where the phrase, "The just shall live by faith," is recorded.

_____

_____

_____

_____

Why is a good testimony important to living a life of faith?

_____
_____
_____
_____

How does faith help you to walk with God?

_____
_____
_____
_____

What verse does the author call "the ring of power"? Why is this verse so important for you as a believer?

_____
_____
_____
_____

How does God reward the faithful person?

_____
_____
_____
_____

Fill in the blanks:

Faith Is Seeing _____ When All The _____
Around You Is _____!

Chapter Two

THE SENDING OF FAITH

FAITH'S OBEDIENCE

As I began this Bible study my intent was to focus on the fact that God is speaking today in our lives and our first response should be one of obedience. This chapter will again shine the light on God's speaking as Paul now introduces Abraham to the lineup of characters in Hebrews 11. It should be noted that Abraham who was called the friend of God was not only a man of faith, but a man of obedience.

> "By faith Abraham obeyed when he was called to go out to the place which he would receive as an inheritance. And he went out, not knowing where he was going." (Hebrews 11:8)

Note that three words found in the first sentence of this verse fulfill the principle of God speaks—I obey. The words are faith, obeyed, and called. God spoke clearly the call for

35

Abraham to leave Ur of the Chaldees. Obedience would take him on a journey to a land he had never seen. Not only had he not seen this land, he had no directions as to the path to take in getting there. Obedience to God's speaking does not require all of the blanks to be filled.

Hence, the call which God spoke to Abraham was received by him in faith. He fulfilled Hebrews 11:6 in that he had to first believe that God existed to receive this word and then he had the full assurance that this God who had spoken would be his rewarder.

Paul uses the name Abraham as he begins his discussion of this Old Testament patriarch. Actually, Abraham's name was Abram at the time of his calling to leave his homeland and make his way to what we know as the Promised Land. He was 75 years old when this command was given. He was 99 when his name was changed to Abraham. The name Abram means father of many. The name Abraham means father of multitudes.

It is in Genesis 12 that we read of his call to leave Ur. In Genesis 15 Abram reminds God that he is still childless. God had just spoken to Abram these words in a vision. "Do not be afraid, Abram. I am your shield, your exceedingly great reward." (Genesis 15:1) These words from God followed right after Abram's rescue of Lot from the army of five kings.

Abram after offering a tithe to Melchizedek had refused to take any reward from the king of Sodom. Abram gave this response to the king of Sodom's offer: "But Abram said to the king of Sodom, 'I have raised my hand to the LORD, God Most High, the Possessor of heaven and earth, that I will take nothing, from a thread to a sandal strap, and that I will not take anything that is yours, lest you should say, 'I have made Abram rich—'" (Genesis 14:22-23)

By faith, Abram having not seen the land in which he would sojourn, obeyed with the confidence that God is a rewarder of all who diligently seek Him. He believed this even before He had heard God speaking this truth to him 24 years later. Only those called by faith can act in faith this way. Obedience is possible because we can trust God to work everything out for our good. So Paul states clearly in Romans 8:28, "And we know that all things work together for good to those who love God, to those who are the called according to His purpose."

You may be thinking at this moment that faith is just not for you. After all, who wants to pull up their tent stakes and head out to a place you've never seen with no particular instructions on how to get there. The lives of these faithful characters seem far above your reach, but I have good news for you.

True faith is always *preceded* by the call of God. Faith is not a leap into the dark. When God speaks you can obey because God's call can always be trusted. He is working all things together for your benefit according to His own purpose.

A look at Genesis 15 once again proves this concept. God tells Abram that He is Abram's reward. He then promises to make his descendants to be like the stars of heaven in number. In Genesis 15:6 we read, "And he (*Abram*) believed in the LORD, and He accounted it to him for righteousness." The ability to believe is the product of faith as it is lived out in obedience. And yet this man of faith could ask just two verses later after God reminded him that He had given Abram all of the Promised Land, "Lord GOD, how shall I know that I will inherit it?" It was at this point that God called for the dividing of the animals into a pathway along which He Himself walked in covenant.

Abraham obeyed God while the call of God was still in his ear. He did not know how God would fulfill the promise yet he obeyed. He did not know how long God would take to perform His word and yet he obeyed. Remember, God called Abram our of Ur at 75 years of age. Isaac, the firstborn of Sarah and him, was born when he was nearly 100. Never forget this truth:

God Is Never Late
But
He's Never Early Either!

True faith is always preceded by the call of God, but true faith must always wait upon God's timing. So often, our hesitancy to respond to God's speaking is not out of fear of what He might say, but because of our impatience in His fulfillment.

Faith never functions with all of the questions settled. Like Abraham, we may be called upon to go even though no one else is going. He had no one to follow in his step of obedience. Faith will often be a lonely journey. Helen Annis wrote these lines of poetry that speaks well to this fact:

> I go on not knowing—
> I would not if I might,
> I'd rather walk in the dark with God
> Than walk alone in the light;
> I'd rather walk by faith with Him
> Than to walk alone by sight.

FAITH'S WALK

God, the Rewarder, promised Abraham that he would receive an inheritance. He told Abram this in Genesis 15 and Paul reiterates it here in Hebrews 11. In both cases, the word means a possession. This possession of land is easily reflected in the opening of Hebrews 11. "Now faith is the substance of things hoped for, the evidence of things not seen." (Hebrews 11:1)

Abraham walked throughout the substance of his faith. In Hebrews 11:9 we read, "By faith he dwelt in the land of promise…" This may seem to be a contradiction. How could he be operating in faith if indeed he was dwelling in the land? Doesn't it cease to be faith once it becomes sight?

You will need to read the rest of this verse to get a better understanding of Abraham's journey of faith. Here's the entire verse: "By faith he dwelt in the land of promise as in a foreign country, dwelling in tents with Isaac and Jacob, the heirs with him of the same promise;" (Hebrews 11:9) Abraham never saw the land of promise as a fulfillment of faith's hope.

It was a type of that which he would finally and ultimately possess, but it was always to him a foreign country. The idea is that he always related to the land wherein he dwelt as somewhat strange and himself nothing more than a stranger in it. This is the only time that the phrase, land of promise, is used in the New Testament. It was the land of promise for it was in that land that God's promise was to be fulfilled. The promise was greater than a mere possession of land. It was a promise of a progeny that would eventually bring forth the Savior.

Abraham spent his days walking in faith while dwelling in tents. Not only did he do so, but the next two generations that followed him are noted as doing so as well. They are called the heirs of the same promise that he had received, so we know that it was not about the land.

They were born in the land. They did not have to go there by faith as their father had. Theirs was the continuation of the faith that had begun when Abraham had believed God and it had been accounted unto him for righteousness. It was all by faith. God spoke—They obeyed.

FAITH'S ASPIRATION

Abraham may have dwelt in tents in a permanent fashion, but this was only in his physical body. Spiritually, Abraham always had his eye cast upward. He serves as a perfect example for the believer. We also have an existence upon this earth for a set period of time, but we spend it with an assurance and aspiration for an eternity that we will spend beyond the confines of time and space—or we should!

Here again you can see Abraham's patience in faith. Not only had he waited nearly a quarter of a century for the birth of Isaac, he waited his entire life for the real inheritance of heaven itself. With all that God had shown him and declared as his, he still walked the land as a pilgrim. He only owned one piece of property outright. He purchased a tomb to lay his dear Sarah in after her death. He later would be placed there as well, but only his physical body remained in the Promised Land. He and Sarah both were welcomed into the city of God. He traded a tent of temporal existence for a city of eternality. He exchanged the sandy floor of a peg-walled tent for the sure foundation of heaven.

Too many believers today are attempting permanence in this life alone. It is an eternal look that eases the grip that we have on the things in this world. One of the best evaluations you can make of your own faith walk is to test the grip you have on the temporal.

I can usually make this judgment easier in other persons' lives than I can in my own. When I am watching the news of some tragedy on television like a flood, tornado, fire, or hurricane, it is easy to determine which of the victims interviewed had a grip on the temporal or the eternal. Their response to the loss in their life exposes this for all to see. The question that I have to ask is what my response would be if I were to experience the same tragedy. I suppose none of us will really know until that part of our lives is tested. But I do know this:

The Best Time To Surrender Is Before You Are Asked To Do So

Real faith always has its eye on the eternal. Faith sets its vision upon the foundation of heaven. It waits for a city whose builder and maker is God (Hebrews 11:10). In doing so, faith finds the hope of substance and the evidence of things not seen with the physical eye.

In his book, *Mere Christianity*, C.S. Lewis wrote, "If you read history you will find that the Christians who did the most for the present world were just those who thought most of the next…It is since Christians have largely ceased to think of the other world that they have become so ineffective in this. Aim at heaven and you will get earth "thrown in.""

I'm not saying that any of us needs a good tragedy to get us refocused, but we surely have become too attached to this world and what it has to offer. Nothing here is permanent. You know this, but you just don't like to think about it. It is easier to think that the trial and tribulation will happen to someone else on the other side of the world. But you know better!

God is speaking today—ease your grip on life. Kenneth W. Osbeck tells the following story of the old gospel hymn, "Trust and Obey" in his book, *Amazing Grace: 366 Inspiring Hymn Stories for Daily Devotions*.

Life can often be a restless, disrupted existence until we give ourselves wholeheartedly to something beyond ourselves and follow and obey it supremely. Such implicit trust in God's great love and wisdom with a sincere desire to follow His leading should be every Christian's goal. Our willingness to trust and obey is always the first step toward God's blessing in our lives.

In 1886 Daniel B. Towner, director of the music department at Moody Bible Institute, was leading the music for evangelist D. L. Moody's series of meetings in Brockton, Massachusetts. A young man rose to give a testimony, saying, "I am not quite sure—but I am going to trust, and I am going to obey." Mr. Towner jotted down this statement and sent it to the Rev. J. H. Sammis, a Presbyterian minister and later a teacher at Moody, who wrote the present five stanzas.

Our responsibility is to trust in that salvation and then to obey its truths. "Trust and Obey" presents a balanced view of a believer's trust in Christ's redemptive work, and it speaks of the resulting desire to obey Him and do His will in our daily lives. Then, and only then, do we experience real peace and joy.

Many of you will be able to sing these words from memory, but if not, here they are for you to read. May they bring a deepening aspiration to live a life of faith.

When we walk with the Lord in the light of His Word, what a glory He sheds on our way! While we do His good will He abides with us still, and with all who will trust and obey.

Not a shadow can rise, not a cloud in the skies, but His smile quickly drives it away; not a doubt nor a fear, not a sigh nor a tear, can abide while we trust and obey.

Not a burden we bear, not a sorrow we share, but our toil He doth richly repay; not a grief nor a loss, not a frown nor a cross, but is blest if we trust and obey.

But we never can prove the delights of His love until all on the altar we lay, for the favor He shows and the joy He bestows are for them who will trust and obey.

Then in fellowship sweet we will sit at His feet, or we'll walk by His side in the way; what He says we will do, where He sends we will go—Never fear, only trust and obey.

Chorus: Trust and obey—for there's no other way to be happy in Jesus—but to trust and obey.

God's speaking—trust and obey!

FAITH'S FRUIT

God does not expect us to simply drift through life driving tent pegs here and there with no real purpose in mind. After Abraham's faith and patience thereby to wait upon

God is detailed in Hebrews 11:8-10, Paul now takes us to the next step in faith: fruitfulness. He introduces Sarah, Abraham's wife, into the equation of faithfulness. "By faith Sarah herself also received strength to conceive seed, and she bore a child when she was past the age, because she judged Him faithful who had promised." (Hebrews 11:11)

Sarah serves as the miraculous mother of Isaac, the son of her old age. Both Sarah and Abraham were well beyond the natural time of being able to produce children. Sarah was 90 years old; Abraham nearing 100. But God who is eternal never takes age into consideration!

A wonderful portrait of faith unfolds in this account of Sarah conceiving at an age beyond all human explanation. Where unbelief is barren, faithfulness is always fruitful. To understand Sarah's part in this demonstration of faith at work, we will need to return once again to the book of Genesis. Here we can get a better understanding of the human side of the equation of faith.

Genesis 18 unfolds the story of Abraham receiving three strangers who came to visit him while he dwelt in his tent (Genesis 18:1). The men asked Abraham, "Where is Sarah your wife?" So he said, "Here, in the tent." (Genesis 18:9) There it is again. We are reminded that Abraham and Sarah were not attached to this world. They both were dwelling in the tent. They both were looking for and expecting something more than this world could offer.

Here is where the storyline gets funny. I know that God has a sense of humor or He simply would have left some biblical characters out of the inspired record. When Abraham received the word from one of the strangers (I believe that "stranger" was a pre-Bethlehem incarnation of Jesus) that Sarah would be delivering a son, Sarah laughed!

I'm so glad that Sarah's response is recorded in scripture for us. Genesis 18:10 informs us that Sarah was in the tent door listening to the interaction between Abraham and the strangers. She is so much like me in faith walk. Though she was dwelling in the tent in the land of promise and waiting for a city yet to come, she was stretching her ear to get the latest news about the here and now. What she learned made her laugh within (Genesis 18:12), but God heard it all.

"For the word of God is living and powerful, and sharper than any two-edged sword, piercing even to the division of soul and spirit, and of joints and marrow, and is a discerner of the thoughts and intents of the heart." (Hebrews 4:12) How is it that we think that we that we can laugh inside our hearts and God not know what's going on within us? Sarah must have been surprised when her laugh was exposed and even more surprised when her denial was rebuked. "But Sarah denied it, saying, 'I did not laugh,' for she was afraid. And He said, 'No, but you did laugh!'" (Genesis 18:15)

I've been in this very place. I have been very comfortable in my tent of faith until challenged to believe what seems impossible. The key to Sarah's response was one little word in the midst of her laughter. The word: shall.

She could have responded in unbelief by asking, "How can this be?" But she used the little word shall. "How shall this be?" leaves room for God to work out the details in the miracle. The process did not matter because the promise was in effect. The procedure did not have to be known because God would fulfill His purpose. The program could be altered because God would give forth the product: a son through whom would come a Savior.

Hebrews 11:11 states clearly that Sarah believed that the fruit of faith would be realized for "she judged Him faithful who had promised." It was not her faith or lack thereof that would bring forth her firstborn. It was God's faithfulness that would result in Isaac's birth.

Remember that God had already changed Abram's name to Abraham long before Isaac was born. A look at the spelling of Abram and Abraham reveals just two letters added: an "h" and an "a". If you put these two letters together you get the little word ha. In other words, God put the "ha" into Abram's life and he became Abraham. Then he gives him a son by miracle and he is named Isaac which means laughter. So Paul describes the fruit of this man's faith in Hebrews 11:12, "...from one man, and him as good as dead, were born as many as the stars of the sky in multitude—innumerable as the sand which is by the seashore."

Sarah may have laughed, but she didn't laugh last or first for that matter. It was God who put the "ha" into this couple's life. He wants to do the same for you. See, this story is funny in a good way. God speaks—Abraham and Sarah obey—and it all turns out to be a happy story!

FAITH'S VISION

We all love a fairy tale ending. Especially those that have a happy ending like was told in the story of Abraham and Sarah. But all of faith's stories do not end with a full revelation of God's purpose. Sometimes life comes and goes and it appears at least for the moment that the happy ending is not going to happen.

Paul informs us in Hebrews 11:13. "These all died in faith, not having received the promises..." What then? Do we give up on faith? Should we resign ourselves to doing our best and coming to the end of this life with the sad disposition of a Solomon? This wise man wrote, "The words of the Preacher, the son of David, king in Jerusalem. 'Vanity of vanities,' says the Preacher; 'Vanity of vanities, all is vanity.' What profit has a man from all his labor in which he toils under the sun? One generation passes away, and another generation comes, but the earth abides forever." (Ecclesiastes 1:1-4) This surely does not sound like a man of faith does it?

Solomon's problem was much like mine and yours is on some days. We get boxed in by the circumstances of life and we honestly begin to think that what we are experiencing in the here and now is all that there is to life. At least we start acting like the stuff we are going through is the new normal—if it is possible to define normal!

This is the place where faith gives us vision. Faith does not need the parameters of this life in which to function. Paul declared that these all died without the promises fulfilled. Yet…

"These all died in faith, not having received the promises, *but having seen them afar off were assured of them, embraced them* and confessed that they were strangers and pilgrims on the earth." (Hebrews 11:13, emphasis mine)

This is the vision of faith. This attribute of faith enables you to see beyond what's happening or even beyond what has happened. The vision of faith is not skewed by the supposed reality of the moment nor by the horror of your history. Faith allows you see the answer while it is yet far away. Faith enables you to be persuaded to the point of embracement.

All of these that Paul has listed up to this point were looking far into the future as if it was right within their grasp.

We know that hundreds of years passed before the fulfillment of the promise occurred, but they did not. They lived each day as if that day would be the moment that faith's vision became their reality.

They *embraced* the promise. This word means that they welcomed, greeted, and offered salutation to the promise with the same warmth as you and I would when we meet someone standing in our very presence. These faithful ones who did not experience the promise in their physical life treated it as real though it was untouched. They all lived out the reality of Hebrews 11:1 in that the vision of faith was both substance and evidence of things not seen.

How did they accomplish this? What was so different about these men and women of faith? The answer to this second question leads to the answer of the first. So, I'll ask it again. What was so different about these men and women of faith?

NOTHING!

That's right! These people were no different from you and I. They were of like passions. They each had their unique set of failings and doubts, but in the end they were just like us. They were a part of fallen humanity. They had all been touched by the deadly influence of sin. So, how did they accomplish this embracing of the promise yet unseen? These all walked through life as strangers and pilgrims. It did not matter their status in life.

Abel was the second son to Adam and Eve. He would have received a smaller inheritance than his brother Cain, but his vision was beyond his birthright. Enoch left this world early in comparison to others in his generation, but he left it all behind to walk home with God.

Noah was called upon to preach to a world that would not listen, but he was able to see the deliverance of his household. Abraham counted grains of sand by day and stars by night seeing children represented in each. Sarah looked beyond her doubting laughter to see the God who alone could bring to pass the birth of a miracle child.

In each case these men and women accomplished a life of faith and lived the vison of faith because they heard God speaking. When God speaks—we can see!

FAITH'S CONFESSION

There is one additional element that brings what some would consider fanciful longing into fulfilled legitimacy. Paul tells us that all of these died in faith not having experienced the validity of the promise, yet they held them as part of their vision of faith. Then he adds the fact that they: "*confessed* that they were strangers and pilgrims on the earth."

True faith is never ashamed to confess. The faithful are never willing to hide behind their present status in life. The faithful mix no words about their belief. Paul adds to their confession this statement: "For those who say such things declare plainly that they seek a homeland." (Hebrews 11:14)

Verses 13 and 14 make it very clear that when faith is at work in a person there will be no chance of silence being present. If you need an evidence of faith having a perfect and ongoing work in your life, it can be found in four words found in these two verse. They are:

Confessed
Say
Declare Plainly

The word confessed means to profess at the same time. It means that these faithful ones could not keep quiet once they realized that God's promises could be counted on as being fulfilled in the here and now even though they had not physically acquired the benefit of the promise. No sooner had God spoken the promise than they began to profess the actuality that they had already acquired the result. **Confession: to profess at the same time**.

Verse 14 then tells us that these faithful Old Testament saints began to say openly what they were believing God for in their lives. The word say is interesting. It is the word *lego* in the original Greek manuscript. Yes, it is the same word that the toy manufacturer has used to name their sets of building blocks. The word means to lay forth systematically. In particular, it speaks of an individual who speaks forth respective of his or her own understanding.

These men and women of old continued to say and to add to their thoughts all that God was saying to them. The more they experienced of God and His promises the more they had to say. Their speech was not some random incoherent mumbo-jumbo. It was a logical and systematic portrayal of the reality of a life that was to be lived apart from and beyond what was seen in the present. **Say: to lay forth a concept systematically**.

Paul leaves no question about their lack of shame in proclaiming their faith. He tells us that they declared it all plainly. The two words "declare plainly" are translated from a single word in the Greek. The word could be translated as emphasized. They emphasized "that they seek a homeland." (Hebrews 11:14) **Declare plainly: to emphasize**.

God's speaking—we talk about it with emphasis!

FAITH'S DEVOTION

When I was a teenager (that was over 40 years ago) very few kids had what could be called anything close to a new car. Most of us drove cars that had been pieced together and were nearly always a left over in the family. Mine was a Rambler. Never mind if there are any of you reading this that knows what a Rambler was. If you do, you've been exposed! You are my age or older!

I set out once to replace the shift mechanism in my 1963 Rambler station wagon. It was a standard on-the-column shift. Because it was worn out and had left me stranded several times, I decided with a friend's help to install a floor shift. It was an easy job to convert the car to this...at least I thought it was.

After a few hours of installing the new floor shift, it was time to take it out for a test drive. I climbed behind the wheel, put the car in reverse, let out the clutch, and proceeded to almost drive into the front wall of the garage in which we had been working! Needless to say, we had to make a few modifications!

I think that we sometimes want to tinker around with faith and presume that we can make it work just for us. Inevitably, however, we discover that faith is not ours to manipulate. It will only operate in one direction according to the Designer's purpose and plan.

After the call of Abraham to leave Ur and travel to the promised land, there was no looking back. It was impossible to shift into another gear and hope to go in the right direction. In every case that faith is seen at work in the Bible it is always propelling people forward. They simply could not go back once the journey of faith had begun. Hebrews 11:15

declares of these early followers of God in faith, "And truly if they had called to mind that country from which they had come out, they would have had opportunity to return."

Faith's devotion prevented them from recalling to their minds or dwelling upon their past home as a memory. The amazing thing is they were completely free to do so, but their commitment to a walk of faith would not allow them to do so. They had the opportunity to turn back. The time was always available for them to make a decision to return to the life of Ur, but they refused to do so.

The word return in the above verse holds the idea of bending. But it also forms a picture of bending repeatedly. It is much like taking a piece of metal and beginning to bend it repeatedly. This piece of metal if left alone is very strong, but when bent back and forth enough times will eventually succumb to the torture and break. These men and women of faith were devoted to the point that they might be bent, but they would never break.

Faith's devotion does not produce a life of ease, but instead it will bring intense pressure into our lives. When you consider all that transpired in the life of Israel you begin to get a better picture of what it means to walk in faith and be devoted to that walk to the end. Yes, it began with Abraham's obedience to faith's call, but his faith and that of his progeny was tested again and again.

He may have dwelt in the land of promise, but it was fraught with constant danger. Famines came which drove Abraham and others in his genealogy to walk away from the promised land. Mistakes were made. Sin was committed. Life altering effects were experienced then and are still rippling through time today. Israel spent 400 years out of the Promised Land and when they returned the land was full of giants. Remember, the only place Israel ever faced giants was in the Promised Land. There were no giants in the wilderness. Giants are always an evidence of walking in faith.

When the Israelites were stranded between the Red Sea and the whole Egyptian army, the command of God was based on faith. He said, "Why do you cry to Me? Tell the children of Israel to go forward." (Exodus 14:15) This command followed Moses' word to the people to stand still and see the salvation of the Lord. (Exodus 14:13) There was nothing inherently wrong in Moses' charge to the people, but faith will never work standing still. There are times that you must go forward even when all of the circumstances indicate an impossibility.

But what if something goes wrong? Don't forget my old Rambler station wagon. I could have left it in neutral and everything would have been fine. I made a decision to put it in gear and even though my work left me going in the wrong direction, this discovery allowed me to reconfigure my work to align it properly with the design of the equipment. Things may appear to be going wrong, but never depart from a devotion to faith. Jesus said, "No one, having put his hand to the plow, and looking back, is fit for the kingdom of God." (Luke 9:62) Paul said of his own walk of faith, "Brethren, I do not count myself to have apprehended; but one thing I do, forgetting those things which are behind and reaching forward to those things which are ahead, I press toward the goal for the prize of the upward call of God in Christ Jesus." (Philippians 3:13-14)

Just like these early believers, Paul concluded that he had his eye looking upward to a higher goal. Jesus said we can't look back. Keep looking back and you will eventually bend enough times to break. The key to not bending to the point of returning is found in a desire for something that is out of this world. They had all the opportunity they needed to return to their old lifestyles, "but now they desire a better, that is, a heavenly country. Therefore God is not ashamed to be called their God, for He has prepared a city for them." (Hebrews 11:16)

True faith directly affects our desires. As faith intensifies, our desire for godly things will increase. They lived in a land flowing with milk and honey, but faith inspired them to seek a *better* home. This word means so much more than a relative comparison of quality. A better home is a home that is stronger, nobler, and a more vigorous residence.

Faith's devotion takes us beyond the temporal to the eternal. The home we seek by faith has at its core an eternal element. It is a home prepared by God Himself. This is why Jesus could comfort His disciples with these words: "Let not your heart be troubled; you believe in God, believe also in Me. In My Father's house are many mansions; if it were not so, I would have told you. I go to prepare a place for you. And if I go and prepare a place for you, I will come again and receive you to Myself; that where I am, there you may be also." (John 14:1-3)

John Calvin, speaking of the text from Hebrews 11 said,

> We are hence to conclude, that there is no place for us among God's children, except we renounce the world, and that there will be for us no inheritance in Heaven, except we become pilgrims on earth.

God's speaking—never look back!

Mileposts

What one thing always precedes faith? How does this one thing keep us from taking a leap into the dark?

_____

_____

_____

_____

Why is it important that we keep an eye on our eternal inheritance rather than an earthly one?

_____

_____

_____

_____

How did the birth of Isaac to Abraham and Sarah further their walk of faith?

_____

_____

_____

_____

Explain how faith can get you beyond whatever circumstances may be happening presently.

_____

_____

_____

_____

How are these three terms defined by the author?

Confessed:_____

Say:_____

Declare plainly:_____

_____

How does faith keep us from returning to our lives as they were before accepting Christ as Lord and Savior?

_____
_____
_____
_____

In what ways does faith affect the desires of your life?

_____
_____
_____
_____

How does a believer relate to the world as a pilgrim?

_____
_____
_____
_____

Fill in the blanks:

God Is Never _____ But He's Never _____ Either!

Chapter Three

THE SACRIFICE OF FAITH

Living in the 21st century does not leave much room for sacrifice. Actually, it does, but 21st century Christians are just not listening very well. God is still speaking about sacrifice; we need only obey what He is speaking to us.

Truthfully, it is more so us American Christians that do not know much about sacrifice. We rise up late on Sunday morning knowing full well that we will arrive to the church in a frenzy. We brave the conditions of our garaged auto and quickly get its interior either cooled or warmed to our personal liking. We drive past half a dozen churches or more to get to the one of our liking. After dropping off our family under a covered walkway, we find the closest parking spot and trudge a few hundred feet to a well-lighted and air conditioned auditorium. When asked how we are doing by the usher our response follows this format, "Ok, I guess!" "It's been one of those weeks!"

Doesn't sound like much sacrifice has gone into our getting to the house of God does it? In many other parts of the world it's a totally different story. The church must meet in secret and the lives of those attending are in direct danger of being taken in martyrdom. The very idea of coming into the Lord's presence like most of us do on a given Sunday would be strange indeed to them. We could learn much about the sacrifice of faith that they are required to offer on a regular basis.

Hebrews 11 begins early on with a call to sacrifice. In Hebrews 11:4 we read, "By faith Abel offered to God a more excellent sacrifice than Cain, through which he obtained witness that he was righteous, God testifying of his gifts; and through it he being dead still speaks." We discussed this fully in chapter one, but now Paul takes the concept of sacrifice to a heightened level of experience. Abel obeyed in offering a lamb. God now requires from Abraham a son.

Remember, I have titled this book, *God's Speaking*. This book was preceded by two others, *God's Leading* and *God's Designing*. My intent in these titles was to bring these attributes of God into the present. It was God who identified Himself to Moses as I Am. I think that we have little problem with believing that God is eternal. We do have a problem with believing that God is eternal right now in the here and now. Somehow we are okay with a God who did great stuff in the past and we know that God will finish all of creation with a bang (2 Peter 3:12.) What we have trouble with is believing that God is leading us today, working out His design in us today, and speaking to us today. There can only be one response:

God Speaks—I obey!

God surely spoke to Abel and it is clear that he obeyed. God accepted both his sacrifice and his act of faith to the point of Abel's own death at the hand of his brother. In both cases it was faith at work. Abel had to believe that God would accept his sacrifice and he had to believe in spite of Cain's negative response and ultimate death blow. Can you say today that you are willing to live a life of sacrifice by faith to this degree? Don't answer that question! I'm not sure any of us can until God speaks directly to us in our particular situation.

But speak God will! He is speaking today as He always has. It is His word that will never pass away though all the earth perish.

> "Heaven and earth will pass away, but My words will by no means pass away." (Matthew 24:35)

FAITH'S TRIAL

Someone once said that three votes are cast on all of our decisions: God casts a vote; the devil casts a vote; and you and I cast the deciding vote. Don't believe this! It might sound good. It might even sound right. But living like this is not a life of faith. It is never left up to you and me. If it were, then we would always be making the wrong choices based on what we know at the moment. Furthermore, we would make choices based on our own comfort, never on a call to sacrifice.

Here's a better statement: **Trials are God's vote of confidence in us**. Now that doesn't fit the current "make me feel good" theology that's floating about these days, but it's the truth. Faith will always be tested at some point. The test, however, is not the point of focus—faith is!

The trial or testing comes for the express purpose of proving faith. When the trial comes, we learn that faith is not optional. Without faith in place then no trial can be survived; no test can be passed. We then can join the Apostle Paul in declaring, "And we know that all things work together for good to those who love God, to those who are the called according to His purpose." (Romans 8:28) Without faith in place we would never be able to say such a thing. We could never see how that God is working all things for good according to His purpose. It is His purpose that is being fulfilled—not our own personal comfort. This is why God could say to Abraham, "'Take now your son, your only son Isaac, whom you love, and go to the land of Moriah, and offer him there as a burnt offering on one of the mountains of which I shall tell you.'" (Genesis 22:2)

God was speaking to Abraham in his day and Abraham's response needed to be exactly what ours should be today: obey! But how can we do this? How could Abraham do it? That is the million dollar question. It is a question that begs an answer, for without one we are going to fight against this entire call of sacrifice.

The answer is not really that difficult. It is wrapped up in the very concept of God speaking. God's speaking produced words. It is these words that are promised to never pass away as Jesus said they would not. It was the spoken word of God that created everything. It was the spoken word of God that had given Abraham the promise of a son. There it is! A word for Abraham! This is what makes faith work—a word from God for me (or in this case Abraham).

Here's how the story unfolds according to Hebrews 11. "By faith Abraham, when he was tested, offered up Isaac, and he who had received the promises offered up his only begotten son, of whom *it was said*, 'In Isaac your seed shall be called,'" (Hebrews 11:17-18, emphasis mine). Do you see it right there in these verses? God tested Abraham by requiring a sacrifice of his son. Abraham was able to respond in faith, because God had already given him a word: "In Isaac your seed shall be called."

This is exactly why Paul could say in his letter to the Romans: "So then faith comes by hearing, and hearing by the word of God." (Romans 10:17) Faith is only possible as a direct result of God speaking. When God speaks we are able to hear based upon His word. Then we are able to respond in faith no matter the circumstance or the call for sacrifice.

A great example of faith being preceded by a word is found in the account of Peter walking on the water—or perhaps I should say walking on the word. You are probably very familiar with this account: "Immediately Jesus made His disciples get into the boat and go before Him to the other side, while He sent the multitudes away. And when He had sent the multitudes away, He went up on the mountain by Himself to pray. Now when evening came, He was alone there. But the boat was now in the middle of the sea, tossed by the waves, for the wind was contrary. Now in the fourth watch of the night Jesus went to them, walking on the sea. And when the disciples saw Him walking on the sea, they were troubled, saying, 'It is a ghost!' And they cried out for fear. But immediately Jesus spoke to them, saying, 'Be of good cheer! It is I; do not be afraid.' And Peter answered Him and said, 'Lord, if it is You, command me to come to You on the water.' So He said, 'Come.' And when Peter had come down out of the boat, he walked on the water to go to Jesus. But when he saw that the wind was boisterous, he was afraid; and beginning to sink he cried out, saying, 'Lord, save me!'" (Matthew 14:22-30)

I want to get beneath the feet of Peter for just a moment and ask a question. Did Peter walk on the water? Yes and no! The scripture says he did, but he could not have without a word from Jesus. Peter made a statement in this episode that does not sound like a confident remark based upon faith. He said, "Lord, *if* it is You." Shouldn't faith be immediately extinguished with the introduction of the tiny word *if*? It would have been, if not for Peter asking Jesus to command him to get out of the boat. Peter went on to say, "command me to come to You on the water." It is at this moment that the words of Jesus set faith free to work in Peter's life. Jesus said, "Come!" That little word was all that was needed.

Again, Romans 10:17, "So then faith comes by hearing, and hearing by the word of God." Peter heard Jesus say come and by faith he got out of the boat. This explains why the others did not. The word was for Peter alone. That is exactly what Romans 10:13 teaches us. The meaning of *word* as found in this verse is a particular word, for a particular person, at a particular time, in a particular situation. If it meant anything less than this, then every person who ever picked up a Bible and read a verse would receive faith, but we know that is not true. Peter had his word and he walked on C-O-M-E. Step by step he walked on the word he had from Jesus. As a by-product he got to walk on water also. It was when he thought he was on the water alone and forgot the word he had from Jesus that he sank.

That brings us back to Abraham.

Abraham would have never begun the three day journey to Mount Moriah, climbed that lonely mountain, or laid his son on the altar without a word from God. Faith is always exercised upon the word. Abraham had the initial word from God that he would have a son, a second word from God that his lineage would proceed through Isaac, and now a new word from God. "Then He said, 'Take now your son, your only son Isaac, whom you love, and go to the land of Moriah, and offer him there as a burnt offering on one of the mountains of which I shall tell you.'" (Genesis 22:2) The very next verse tells us that Abraham rose early the next morning and proceeded in his step of obedience. (Genesis 22:3)

Two lessons can be learned when it comes to the testing or trial of your faith. First, the test will involve that which is dear to us. Second, when the trial comes, obey immediately.

This command of God for Abraham to offer up his son is not easy for us to wrap our arms around. It flies in the face of what we want to believe about God. Yet Abraham obeyed without question. This did not mean, however, that Abraham did not struggle with the decision. Let me explain...

I know that the few verses that entail this entire transaction on Mount Moriah leave us with the impression that Abraham simply walked up the mountain, bound his son's hands and feet, laid him on the altar, and drew his knife. This is what we read in Genesis 22:3-10. But I cannot believe that Abraham was less than a man of like passions as we are. Why else would God include his story with all of the sordid details as well as the highlights? Yes, Abraham performed admirably, but he also had his moments of failure. We all do.

If I may, I would like to fill in a few of the gaps as I might imagine them. I am not changing the inspired words of the text. I just have a vivid imagination!

First, let's get some of the chronology straight in our minds. When God commanded Abraham to offer Isaac he was probably about 120 years old. Isaac most likely was around 20. The scripture calls him a lad. The Hebrew word translated as lad can be indicative of anyone from a child to an adolescent, but at its root it means to growl and shake the mane as in a lion's roar. I prefer to think of Isaac as being well able to resist this whole episode, but he did not. There were two faiths being tested on the mountain that day: Abraham's and Isaac's. Indeed, the day would come when Isaac would need the lessons learned on the mountain.

Isaac was old enough to clearly understand the sacrificial act of worship. On the way up the mountain he said to his father, "'My father!' And he said, 'Here I am, my son.' Then he said, 'Look, the fire and the wood, but where is the lamb for a burnt offering?'" (Genesis 22:7) Abraham's response is fraught with meaning. "'My son, God will provide for Himself the lamb for a burnt offering.' So the two of them went together." (Genesis 22:8)

Clearly Abraham was convinced that God would intercede. The meaning in this context is that God would provide a substitute for Isaac. The greater meaning is that God ultimately provided a substitute for all of us. Still deeper is the thought that Abraham was saying to Isaac that God Himself would be the sacrifice. Indeed He was in Christ Jesus!

Do not let the last word of verse 8 be missed. This verse concludes with the fact that the two of them went together. The idea here is that Abraham and Isaac were in complete unity. They walked the trail to the top of Moriah as one unit. Though they were there as individuals, they acted as one in the faith. Maybe this was what Jude had in mind when he wrote, "Beloved, while I was very diligent to write to you concerning our common salvation, I found it necessary to write to you exhorting you to contend earnestly for the faith which was once for all delivered to the saints." (Jude 1:3) Jude speaks of a common faith and *the* faith that is delivered to *all* the saints.

The two men, father and son, now reach the summit of the mount. An altar is constructed and the wood laid in order upon it. Now comes the strategic moment. The instant we all shudder to think would ever happen to us. God is requiring the apple of our eye. The treasure of our heart is being required. The decision must be made.

In my mind's eye, I see no struggle. Isaac is not looking for a way of escape. He lays himself upon the altar as a willing act of obedience. His father binds him there with loving hands and tear stained cheeks. Surely Paul must have had this scene in mind when he wrote, "I beseech you therefore, brethren, by the mercies of God, that you present your bodies a living sacrifice, holy, acceptable to God, which is your reasonable service. And do not be conformed to this world, but be transformed by the renewing of your mind, that you may prove what is that good and acceptable and perfect will of God." (Romans 12:1-2)

Isaac presented himself as a son of obedience. He was acting out of obedience to his earthly father and his heavenly Father simultaneously. Maybe as you consider this account of faith you are wondering what God is going to ask of you. The question is not what God is asking you to surrender in sacrifice, but who. It is you that He is desiring upon the altar. Romans 12:1 speaks to *you* that *you* present your body as a living sacrifice. And this is where the real problem crops up in our everyday lives. We are *living* sacrifices. Jesus has already died for us so we might live life more abundantly. It is the living part that causes us to err. Living sacrifices had a tendency to crawl off of the altar. This may be why Jesus told His disciples, "'If anyone desires to come after Me, let him deny himself, and take up his cross daily, and follow Me. For whoever desires to save his life will lose it, but whoever loses his life for My sake will save it.'" (Luke 9:23-24)

We must daily get back on the altar. We must daily deny ourselves. Crosses are for dying upon not for glorifying self. If you will be saved you must be lost to self. It's time to get on the altar!

If this were a movie, the background music would be reaching a crescendo about now. We would be on the edge of our seat with the expectation that something both horrible and mysterious was about to happen. A father is about to sacrifice his son. He is doing so at the command of a God who cannot be seen. It is a glorious act of faith.

The mid-morning sun is now shining brightly upon this pair. Father stands next to the son of submission. Abraham gently places his hand over the eyes of his son and with determined purpose draws the knife from the sheath at his side. The son of promise breathes rapidly knowing that his life in this world is about to end.

Abraham lifts the knife toward heaven and perhaps whispers one more prayer. "Anytime now, Lord. Is this not enough? Have I not obeyed your every command?" His thoughts may have rushed back to the time that he asked God for an heir. Maybe he wished he had not. His arm tenses as he prepares to thrust the blade deep into the heart of his son. The sun glints upon the blade. His eyes leave the face of his son and he looks upward beyond the blue sky seeking the face of God, wanting desperately to hear God speaking.

The knife leaves its highest altitude and with all of Abraham's strength makes its way to the rising chest of Isaac. Its sharpened point now touches his garment...a single thread is pricked...another nanosecond and the blade will pierce the heart and life will end for Isaac...and then...

God speaks!

"'Abraham, Abraham!'"

"So he said, 'Here I am.'"

"And He said, "Do not lay your hand on the lad, or do anything to him; for now I know that you fear God, since you have not withheld your son, your only son, from Me." (Genesis 22:11-12)

All of us issue forth a collective gasp at the averted tragedy. Relief washes over us all and with rejoicing the intensified background music is replaced with the bleating of a sheep caught by its horns in the thicket next to the altar and within the hearing of both father and son. (Genesis 22:13)

The ram is killed and offered up in Isaac's stead and Abraham called the place where all of this took place, Jehovah-Jireh, The-Lord-Will-Provide. And the two came back down the mountain as Abraham had told his servants they would. For by faith he had concluded that God would be faithful to His own word. Faithful, even if he had to raise Isaac from the dead. As a matter of fact, Hebrews 11:19 tells us that Abraham had already considered Isaac dead before he had ever ascended the mountain.

Remember that I told you there were two things that could be learned from the trial of faith. The trial will always involve that which is dear to us and we should be ready to obey immediately when called upon to do so. Well, there is a third thing also. It is what makes the first two possible for us to survive. Never forget:

God Is Never Late
But
He's Never Early Either!

Just as He showed up on the mountain for Abraham and Isaac, He will show up for you: On time—Every time!

God's Speaking—Obey now!

FAITH'S BLESSINGS

Abraham was blessed because he obeyed God. He obeyed God even though he did not understand all that God was commanding. Faith operates even when we cannot comprehend what is happening in the moment and even when we could never imagine how God is going to fulfill His own word. The promise of God was proven through Abraham's obedience. Though he could not understand he could still obey. Many are waiting for God to prove Himself; God is waiting on many just to obey.

This one act of obedience on Abraham's part caused a chain reaction of faith that permeated generations to come. The next verse in Hebrews 11 tell the story. "By faith Isaac blessed Jacob and Esau concerning things to come. By faith Jacob, when he was dying, blessed each of the sons of Joseph, and worshiped, leaning on the top of his staff. By faith Joseph, when he was dying, made mention of the departure of the children of Israel, and gave instructions concerning his bones." (Hebrews 11:20-22)

Jay Rouse wrote the words to this song about passing the faith along. It really tells the story of the generations that followed Abraham.

Passin' the faith along to my brother, passin' the faith along / Helpin' to build the faith of another, passin' the faith along / Sharin' a word of faith with another, helpin' to make him strong / Passin' the faith along to my brother, passin' the faith along

The runner of a relay, finds in his baton / The purpose for the runnin' and the strength to carry on / We hold within our grasp, the faith that makes us strong / And like the relay runner, we seek to pass it on

Countless generations of saints have come and gone / A spark ignites into a flame, and the faith continues on / A challenge for the young, and assurance for the old / The faith burns ever brighter, each time my story's told

Passin' the faith along to my brother, passin' the faith along / Helpin' to build the faith of another, passin' the faith along / Sharin' a word of faith with another, helpin' to make him strong / Passin' the faith along to my brother, passin' the faith along

The faith that we have is not intended for our safe keeping. We are to pass it along as directed by the Lord. Like Abraham, we may be called upon to offer what is dear to us back to Him in surrender. Job declared, "Naked I came from my mother's womb, and naked shall I return there. The LORD gave, and the LORD has taken away; blessed be the name of the LORD." (Job 1:22) We do not know what influence Job's response had on the generations that followed.

Abraham's response would have been, "The Lord has given, but He wants me to give him back." That is the work of faith. It is not God's demand that gets the attention of the next generation, but our response to His demand in faith that makes the difference. Faith allows the promise to be passed to our children and on to our children's children. Remember it was Isaac's faith that was tested on the mountain as well. It was because of this he was able to bless Jacob and Esau concerning the things to come. (Hebrews 11:20)

The amazing thing about passing our faith along, and the blessing that accompanies it, is that it accomplishes great things in spite of the person who receives the blessing. Jacob is a prime example of this. He was not a remarkable specimen of faith in many cases.

One of the incredible characteristics of faith is that it allows the promises of God to always be intact even in the face of our weaknesses. Hebrews 11:20 states that the blessing of faith was bestowed upon Jacob and Esau. A look back at the birth records will disclose that Esau was the firstborn and it would seem logical that faith's blessing be passed first to Esau and then to Jacob, but here is where the weakness of man enters the picture.

Genesis 27 recounts the conniving and trickery of both Jacob and his mother Rebekah. Isaac being old and frail had lost most of his eyesight. He called his oldest son Esau and asked him to go into the field to hunt for game that could be prepared into a savory meal before his death. His plan was to bestow upon Esau the blessing of the family birthright.

Rebekah instructed Jacob to prepare a lamb with the same savory spices, deceive his old father, and thereby steal the blessing. Actually, Esau had already traded Jacob the birthright for a simple bowl of stew (Genesis 25:29-34). Soon the deed was done. Jacob had completed the deception and Esau's despising of his birthright was fully exposed.

Needless to say, all was not well between these brothers and Jacob flees for his life spending the better part of two decades working for his uncle Laban. Here again, Jacob uses his cunning to become a rich man before being driven out by his uncle. He makes his way back home with two wives, children, servants, and herds of animals. Word of his arrival precedes him and Esau comes to meet him along the way (Genesis 32:6).

In all of this God continued to bless Jacob. You may ask why this should be and you would be asking a good question. The answer is not found in our sense of justice, but in God's purpose being fulfilled. Remember, God is never late, but He's never early either. All of His ways are righteous. His ways are beyond our ways. His thoughts are greater than ours. "Oh, the depth of the riches both of the wisdom and knowledge of God! How unsearchable are His judgments and His ways past finding out! For who has known the mind of the LORD? Or who has become His counselor?" (Romans 11:33-34)

All of the time Jacob thought he was in control, He was not. God was bringing him to the place of total faith so that He might bless him. The journey may have been long and convoluted, but he arrived at the place of God's choosing at the appointed hour. He also arrived alone. Alone in our faith is the part that most of us resist, but it is when we are alone with God that the greatest blessing unfolds upon us.

Jacob now finds himself facing the prospect of meeting his brother. A brother whom he must have assumed still had a deep vendetta and a desire to settle an old score. It did not look good for Jacob and he faced this trial like he had faced many others. He attempted to contrive a remedy.

I can relate to this. I find it easier to trust the bank than seek the riches of God. I will rely on a doctor before I ask the Great Physician. I will take a piece of paper that I can't read to a pharmacist that I do not know. He will dispense pills I have never seen and give me explicit instructions on how they should be taken. I do so with unfailing faith that they are not poison to my system and trust that by the time the bottle runs out of pills I will be well. But…I question God when He asks me to trust Him in the smallest of issues in life. Go figure!

Jacob first tries to bribe his way back into Esau's good graces. Then he divides his troop into two parts and sends them one after the other across the river assuming that at least one of them might make it to safety. He, on the other hand, remains behind to see what might become of his super-duper plan. That brings us to Genesis 32:21, "So the present went on over before him, but he himself lodged that night in the camp."

He himself…

Now God could work with him! He had been able to hide behind his mama, work for his uncle, get rich by his own schemes, labor for the hand of two wives, have children, and make his way back home all on his own. None of this impressed God. God needed him by himself and now God had him exactly where He wanted him.

It might do you good to stop right now and ask God if all that you've been experiencing has just been God getting you all alone. God wants to give you faith's blessing, but it will only come when you are alone with Him and He alone can receive all of the glory for the gift.

Before we look at the story of Jacob's encounter with God, see how Paul speaks of Jacob's life in Hebrews 11 and summarizes it in one single verse. "By faith Jacob, when he was dying, blessed each of the sons of Joseph, and worshiped, leaning on the top of his staff." (Hebrews 11:21)

Note that none of the trials nor the tricks of Jacob's life are detailed. He simply comes to the end of his life and blesses the sons of Joseph. All that he endured and all that he had brought upon himself led to his ability to pass the faith along. But there is one little addition that is added to his story of faith. He worshipped God leaning on the top of his staff. Why would the Spirit of God move upon Paul to include what might otherwise be a side note in Jacob's life? The answer is found once again back in the book of Genesis.

"Then Jacob was left alone; and a Man wrestled with him until the breaking of day. Now when He saw that He did not prevail against him, He touched the socket of his hip; and the socket of Jacob's hip was out of joint as He wrestled with him.

And He said, 'Let Me go, for the day breaks.'

But he said, 'I will not let You go unless You bless me!'

So He said to him, 'What is your name?'

He said, 'Jacob.'

And He said, 'Your name shall no longer be called Jacob, but Israel; for you have struggled with God and with men, and have prevailed.'

Then Jacob asked, saying, 'Tell me Your name, I pray.'

And He said, 'Why is it that you ask about My name?' And He blessed him there.

So Jacob called the name of the place Peniel: 'For I have seen God face to face, and my life is preserved.' Just as he crossed over Penuel the sun rose on him, and he limped on his hip.

Therefore to this day the children of Israel do not eat the muscle that shrank, which is on the hip socket, because He touched the socket of Jacob's hip in the muscle that shrank." (Genesis 32:24-32)

I love this story! Maybe I love it so much because I've been there before. How about you? Have you ever wrestled with God in the night? Have you had your character changed by a touch from God? Have others noticed a certain limp in your walk that makes you different from others who claim the name of Jesus? I certainly hope so!

Alone with a Man. I believe this man was none other than Jesus Himself. The same Jesus who had appeared to Abraham to bring the news of Jacob's father's birth was now appearing to Jacob himself. Where Abraham yielded, Jacob fought. Where Abraham had believed God, Jacob made demands of God. Where Abraham understood that he was to be a blessing because he was blessed, Jacob sought a blessing to add to his already overly blessed life. Nevertheless, God dealt with both of these men right where they were. He will deal with you the same way…right where you are in life.

As Jacob wrestled with Jesus through the night, it might have appeared to some that the bout would end in a draw.

But the truth is, God always wins. He wins, because He knows the tender spot in our life. For Abraham it was his love for Isaac. For Jacob it was in his misconceived idea of his own strength. God required a touch upon the heart of Abraham, He required a touch upon the hip of Jacob.

I cannot help but think of the commercial that has been on television for so many years now, when I think of this touch by the finger of Jesus upon the hip of Jacob. Had Jacob not been able to cling helplessly to Jesus, he most certainly would have cried out, "Help! I've fallen and I can't get up!"

But cling he did. He clung because he could. Truly we have a friend that is closer than a brother (Proverbs 18:24). Never fear the disabling touch of the Master, for in that moment you shall find that He is ready to bear you and your burden. So, this same Jesus said to us in Matthew's gospel, "Come to Me, all you who labor and are heavy laden, and I will give you rest. Take My yoke upon you and learn from Me, for I am gentle and lowly in heart, and you will find rest for your souls. For My yoke is easy and My burden is light." (Matthew 11:28-30)

In this moment of absolute dependence, the desire for the blessing of faith is born and the transfer thereof is bestowed. Jacob, clinging to Jesus yet clinging to his old nature, demands a blessing. At this very moment (not a second late nor a second early) Jesus responds with what may seem an out of place question. "What is your name?"

No one reading this would ever believe that Jesus did not know whom He was with that night. It was not Jesus who needed to hear the response to this question. It was Jacob!

"Jacob."

A one word response filled with all the ugliness of his past. Jacob: trickster, schemer, deceiver. In this moment Jacob saw himself for who he really was. It is only in such a moment that we will accept the truth of our nothingness and come to understand His fullness. We have nothing to bring. He has all we need!

In an instant Jacob was changed. The answer to his demand for a blessing was a change of character. Jacob became Israel. Jacob, the heel grabber (Genesis 25:26), became the God holder. Jacob, the supplanter, became the strong man of God. It all happened with a touch that Jacob never got over for the rest of his life.

That single touch by the finger of Jesus showed up in a lifetime of limping. The next morning when he rejoined his family he limped on his hip (Genesis 32:31). So much was his life marked by this occasion that the nation of Israel would not eat the meat that came from the hip of an animal in remembrance of this encounter with God. This moment in the early hours of the morning stayed with Jacob to the day of his death. The blessing of faith that he received in the touch of Jesus, he passed along to his children and grandchildren. So it is noted in Hebrews 11:21 that he worshiped leaning upon the top of his staff.

The blessing of faith left him leaning on Jesus. So the words of this old hymn remind us:

> What a fellowship, what a joy divine,
> Leaning on the Everlasting Arms!
> What a blessedness, what a peace is mine,
> Leaning on the Everlasting Arms!

O how sweet to walk in this pilgrim way,
Leaning on the Everlasting Arms!
O how bright the path grows from day to day,
Leaning on the Everlasting Arms!

What have I to dread, what have I to fear,
Leaning on the Everlasting Arms,
I have peace complete with my Lord so near,
Leaning on the Everlasting Arms!

Leaning, leaning,
Safe and secure from all alarms;
Leaning, leaning,
Leaning on the Everlasting Arms

So is it really that important to pass our faith along? Will it matter if one generation is skipped? It would have mattered greatly if Jacob had not by faith blessed Joseph. As we shall see, it was Joseph's faith that preserved an entire nation for 400 years in a foreign land.

Over and again Hebrews 11 summarizes a life of faith in one short verse. So it is with the account of Joseph. He is introduced in Hebrews 11:22 in this way: "By faith Joseph, when he was dying, made mention of the departure of the children of Israel, and gave instructions concerning his bones." As with his father Jacob, his life unfolds only at the end. Herein lies a great truth. It is not our lives that really are important. It's not about me and you as much as it is about the faith that is at work in us. All that we are at present, at least all that we are that matters, is because faith has been at work in us.

Now one might conclude that Paul did not include the full discourse of these lives for sake of space or perhaps he assumed that the readers of this letter would know the background of these characters. Both of these assumptions might be true, but here we are in the 21st century and there are people who do not know the story of these patriarchs. Some people in this world are not privileged to have been brought up going to Sunday School, sitting under biblical preaching, or even own an entire copy of God's word. What of these people? Could they gain insight from a single verse about a man's life of faith? Surely, the Spirit of God directed these concise statements, because it's all about Him and not about us. It is His gift of faith that makes even one verse about us possible much less an entire history.

But...we are blessed! We have the history of these individuals to look back upon and from their pasts we can gain a deeper appreciation for the lives of faith which they lived. Once again we take a trip back into the book of Genesis and find the amazing story of Joseph, a true man of faith.

How can a man reach his dying moment and with full confidence look ahead 400 years to see an outcome that belies the present circumstances? How can a living and breathing man give hope to others through instructions about his own dried up bones? The answer is faith!

Circumstances were the least of Joseph's concern. I doubt that any of us could come up with a tragic story in our life that would compare with all that Joseph endured. He was sold into slavery by his own brothers because of their jealousy. He was seduced and falsely accused by Potiphar's wife resulting in his imprisonment. He was forgotten and betrayed by the butler and the baker who had promised to remember him after their release from prison. He ruled alongside the pagan Pharaoh while his family suffered a famine in the land. He watched with grief as his brothers came seeking help in Egypt not knowing his own identity.

Certainly sounds like a soap opera to me! Honestly, it sounds very familiar to the drama that happens in all of our lives: jealousy, false accusation, betrayal, and so much more. Yet in and through all of this Joseph remained faithful. A life in Egypt never changed Joseph's longing for the Promised Land.

Joseph had been blessed by the passing along of faith. He knew by experience what the Apostle Paul hundreds of years later wrote. "But we have this treasure in earthen vessels, that the excellence of the power may be of God and not of us. We are hard-pressed on every side, yet not crushed; we are perplexed, but not in despair; persecuted, but not forsaken; struck down, but not destroyed—always carrying about in the body the dying of the Lord Jesus, that the life of Jesus also may be manifested in our body. For we who live are always delivered to death for Jesus' sake, that the life of Jesus also may be manifested in our mortal flesh. So then death is working in us, but life in you. And since we have the same spirit of faith, according to what is written, "I believed and therefore I spoke," we also believe and therefore speak, knowing that He who raised up the Lord Jesus will also raise us up with Jesus, and will present us with you. For all things are for your sakes, that grace, having spread through the many, may cause thanksgiving to abound to the glory of God. Therefore we do not lose heart. Even though our outward man is perishing, yet the inward man is being renewed day by day. For our light affliction, which is but for a moment, is working for us a far more exceeding and eternal weight of glory, while we do not look at the things which are seen, but at the things which are not seen. For the things which are seen are temporary, but the things which are not seen are eternal." (2 Corinthians 4:7-18)

Paul said he did not look at things which are seen, but at things which are not seen. This sure sounds like his words rephrased in Hebrews 11:1. "Now faith is the substance of things hoped for, the evidence of things not seen." Surely, if Paul is indeed the author of Hebrews, he would have thought about all that Joseph would have seen in his life. He saw a pit, Potiphar, prison, and Pharaoh. Yet at the end of his life he only saw the unseen: **The Promise!**

Joseph knew by faith that God would not leave his children in Egypt forever. With the confidence of faith at work even up to the last days of his life, he gave instructions for the removal of his bones from Egypt. He would not die without passing the faith along to his brothers. He would not die without looking over into the Promised Land for his final resting place.

"So Joseph dwelt in Egypt, he and his father's household. And Joseph lived one hundred and ten years. Joseph saw Ephraim's children to the third generation. The children of Machir, the son of Manasseh, were also brought up on Joseph's knees. And Joseph said to his brethren, 'I am dying; but God will surely visit you, and bring you out of this land to the land of which He swore to Abraham, to Isaac, and to Jacob.' Then Joseph took an oath from the children of Israel, saying, "God will surely visit you, and you shall carry up my bones from here." So Joseph died, being one hundred and ten years old; and they embalmed him, and he was put in a coffin in Egypt." / "And Moses took the bones of Joseph with him, for he had placed the children of Israel under solemn oath, saying, 'God will surely visit you, and you shall carry up my bones from here with you.'" (Genesis 50:22-26; Exodus 13:19)

Joseph's life comes to an end without any word of complaint against God. There was no charge of unfairness. He never said, "Why me?" He passed the faith along faithfully. These final verses in Genesis tell us that the great grandchildren of Joseph were brought up upon his knees (Genesis 50:23). This phrase, *brought up*, carries the idea of serving as a midwife. Joseph was so integrally involved in the upbringing of his children, grandchildren, and great children it was as if he had birthed them all himself. He invested himself fully in passing the faith along. How about you? Are you actively seeking opportunities to make sure that the generations that follow you will still be serving Christ long after you are gone?

Joseph, like Abel, had a faith that was still speaking though he was dead. His testimony was so sure that even with the passing of 400 years the oath taken by his heirs was fulfilled. As the children of Israel left Egypt they bore the bones of their father Joseph to the Promised Land.

God's speaking—now pass it along.

Mileposts

In what ways does God use trials to increase our faith?

_____

_____

_____

_____

Why is it important to have a word from God before you
take a step of faith?

_____

_____

_____

_____

How can you pass your faith on to the next generation?

_____

_____

_____

_____

What did Joseph ask the Hebrew people to do upon their
deliverance? How was this an act of faith?

_____

_____

_____

_____

Fill in the blanks:

Trials are God's _____ of _____

Chapter Four

THE SURRENDER OF FAITH

There is a subtle division that occurs at this point in Hebrews 11. With the principle of faith settled in the first twenty-two verses, the text takes on a much more practical air. This adds to my conviction that Paul is the author of this book. He uses the same format in his other letters. He establishes a series of deep theological truths and then he gives the practical aspect of living out these truths in the context of everyday life.

Having concluded a continual referral back to Genesis in the first three chapters of this book, it is time to move on to Exodus. Between Hebrews 11:22 and Hebrews 11:23 four hundred years transpire. Like the small amount of white space that you see in your Bible between these two verses, so time passes so very quickly. These years are spent by the children of Israel in super oppressive slavery. They cried out to God for a deliverer and He heard them. Will faith be found to have survived such an ordeal? Is it possible to still hear God speaking after so long? Thank God it is possible!

Hebrews 11:23 begins after 400 years of slavery with the same words that had told the end of Joseph's life. "By faith Moses, when he was born, was hidden three months by his parents, because they saw he was a beautiful child; and they were not afraid of the king's command."

By faith! What words of comfort and hope these are when all is dark and the forecast is only for more darkness. My pastor used to tell me when times seemed forlorn, "Son, it's getting gloriously darker!" I believe this more today than ever, don't you?

In all of the previous verses of Hebrews 11, each person represented operated by faith in their own lives and then it was passed along to the next. As we have already discussed in the last chapter, one of the last acts of these men and women was to pass their faith along near the end of their lives. Now we are presented with Moses: the long expected deliverer. But he is not a grown adult. He is not a man on a mountain top offering his son. He is not alone with God wrestling in the night. He is not exiled to Egypt. He is a baby and it is his parents' faith that is at work in his life even before he was accountable for his own faithfulness.

FAITH'S SECRET

Every mother looks over their newborn and after careful examination dreams a little of this child's future. Thoughts of grand achievement, presidential aspirations, and scientific accomplishment may be just a few of her imaginings. But what of this newborn's spiritual exploits? Where will the purpose of God take this child over the course of a lifetime? Can a parent take steps in the days of a child's infancy that will shape the outcome of spiritual maturity? The parents of Moses sure did.

Moses could not have been born at a worse time. Because the number of the Israelite slaves was increasing dramatically, an edict had come from Pharaoh that all of the male children of the Israelites were to be thrown into the Nile River (Exodus 1:22). These babies literally were fed to the crocodiles.

The parents of Moses did their best to hide their son from the hands of the executioner, but growing baby boys can only be kept quiet for so long. The time came for a decision that was based entirely upon faith. From his birth, they knew that Moses was destined to be used by God. Both the Hebrew text in Exodus and this verse from the Greek in Hebrews 11:23 translates Moses as being a beautiful child. Initially, this means nothing more than the fact that Moses was fair of complexion, joyful, well-tempered, etc. But we gain a deeper insight in its meaning from the words of the first martyr, Stephen.

As Stephen was speaking in the defense of his faith, he gave a recounting of Israel's history. In Acts 7:20 he states this about Moses: "At this time Moses was born, and *was well pleasing to God*; and he was brought up in his father's house for three months." (emphasis mine) This is very interesting that Stephen who by faith died by stoning would be instructed in his final minutes of life to disclose this little nugget of description about Moses. Even more interesting is that he is noted as being well pleasing to God. From Hebrews 11:6, we know that without faith it is impossible to please God. As discussed earlier, God gives us this very faith so that we might be pleasing unto Him and that He then might be the rewarder of those who seek Him.

There can be no doubt that Stephen was speaking under the inspiration of the Holy Spirit, therefore, God must have already given to Moses the gift of faith from his very birth.

Moses certainly proves this to be the case as we see his life unfold through the Exodus account of Israel's history. But long before he appears on the scene as the one who would lead Israel out of captivity, we see the hand of God at work in Moses' own deliverance.

As in most cases where faith is found to be at work, it is not only the faith holder's life that is affected, but others with whom that person comes into contact. If we continue on the grounds that Moses was well pleasing to God. then we know that faith was at work. That faith had a profound impact upon his parents, his sister, the daughter of Pharaoh, and the entire nations of both the Egyptians and the Israelites. Faith is much more powerful than most of us realize.

The faith at work in Moses' life moved his parents to respond with godly fear in response to the horrific command of Pharaoh. Hebrews 11:23 clearly states that they were not afraid of Pharaoh's command. The word translated as *afraid* is the same word from which we derive our English word phobia. The circumstances in which they found themselves had no power to create alarm or fright. They refused to be frozen because of fear. Something had to be done, so it was done. Oh, for Christians who would act in this day out of the standard of faith instead of the sense of fear. Whatever your phobia is today surrender it to Christ! The wise man Solomon said, "The fear of man brings a snare, but whoever trusts in the LORD shall be safe." (Proverbs 29:25)

Hebrews tells us that the parents of Moses were working in concert to hide Moses. The book of Exodus only speaks of his mother. I am sure that both worked together, but as we all know, it is a mother that can be the most easily roused when the defense or safety of her children is at stake. Moms are willing to make the sacrifices needed for the protection and the promotion of their kids.

We all have seen athletes stand before the world's stage as they accept commendation for their accomplishments. No one is ever surprised when these words are heard, "Thanks mom!" It's not that dads don't play a vital role; they should. It is just that mothers are the ones that see beyond the bumps and bruises of life and behold the finished product that no one else can see.

I have a very active imagination. I like to use that imagination when it comes to biblical stories. My intent is not to change the account nor look for a different outcome. I just enjoy imagining some of the behind the scene details. For example, if we just read the text about Moses in Exodus 2, you would assume that Moses was hidden for three months; then on day 91 everyone rushed about trying to build a basket that would bear him away to safety on the Nile River. I imagine it differently.

My mind's eye sees Jochebed, the mother of Moses, preparing for the ark of bulrushes even before he was born. She knew the danger that might come. If this child of hers was a male child, then he was under condemnation. He had been under condemnation from the moment of his conception. Even so with us, for scripture says, "Behold, I was brought forth in iniquity, and in sin my mother conceived me." (Psalm 51:5) We all come into this world condemned. We all are in need of saving, because we are born under the condemnation of sin. Like Jochebed working on an ark of salvation for Moses, God provided a Savior for us before the foundation of the world. "He indeed was foreordained before the foundation of the world, but was manifest in these last times for you who through Him believe in God, who raised Him from the dead and gave Him glory, so that your faith and hope are in God." (1 Peter 1:20-21)

Yes, I can see Jochebed making a daily journey to the river's edge and choosing only the finest reeds. One after another she wove them together, making sure that each seam was as tight as possible. She sealed each intersecting weave with a tear and thought secretly by faith of the day when she would place her little baby boy in this makeshift vessel and set it afloat upon the crocodile infested waters of the Nile. Only a mother's handiwork could provide such an ark of salvation. Only a mother's ear could hear the still small voice of God speaking of her yet unborn child. "He shall be a beautiful child. He shall be well pleasing to Me!"

And finally, as always occurs in the journey of faith, the day comes when faith must risk everything. The baby could be hidden no longer. The little ship of salvation was taken out of hiding and prepared for a journey of faith into the unknown. "But when she could no longer hide him, she took an ark of bulrushes for him, daubed it with asphalt and pitch, put the child in it, and laid it in the reeds by the river's bank." (Exodus 2:3) Again, we see that faith never operates in isolation for the next verse in this same chapter says, "And his sister stood afar off, to know what would be done to him." (Exodus 2:4)

Here's where my imagination really gets going full speed, but before I let you take a look into my mind, let's take a look at the provision of God. "Then the daughter of Pharaoh came down to bathe at the river. And her maidens walked along the riverside; and when she saw the ark among the reeds, she sent her maid to get it." (Exodus 2:5)

One little word jumps out immediately: **then**. Remember, God is never late, but He's never early either. The daughter of Pharaoh shows up for her bath—**then**! Not an hour earlier; not ten minutes later. **Right then**!

Somewhere up river his mother had gently laid him in the watertight ark and shoved it away from the bank. Her tears splashing down sent ripples out to push her son even further away, and then caught by the current she watched it bobbing its way around the bend—to the unknown. There she stood and prayed by faith that her efforts would be rewarded by the God who is a rewarder of all who diligently seek Him.

The mouths of the crocodiles were shut like the mouths of lions would be years later while Daniel slept peacefully in their den. Little Moses would have cooed and gurgled as his makeshift boat gently rocked him. The waters of the Nile, under the direction of God's hand, guided his little boat to the exact spot where the richest woman in Egypt was about to disrobe for her dip in the river. As if God Himself were on board with paddle in hand, the little vessel comes to rest within the sight of Pharaoh's daughter.

And then it happened! As she peeked into this basket covered with dark sticky asphalt and pitch, she saw a most beautiful sight. A baby boy delivered, as it were, miraculously out of the river. I imagine at this moment God dispatched an angel with a most curious responsibility. God speaks to the angel and says, "Go pinch that baby!" On cue, in the nick of time, the baby cries (Exodus 2:6).

I don't know many women who could resist the urge and neither could the daughter of Pharaoh! She had compassion on him and her heart was melted. So begins the life of Moses in the realm of royalty!

God's speaking—get ready for a change.

Faith's Selection

It will never be determined on this side of eternity the full impact that parents have on the spiritual lives of their children. The evidence is clear, however, when the histories of families are studied, that faith either has or has not been passed along to following generations. There is no more important decision for parents to make than to be sure that their faith has been passed along to their children.

Now every generation is ultimately responsible for selecting faith or surrendering to the world's allurements, but the decision to hear God's voice and follow His will is made easier when a solid background of faith has been established. This is why you see generations of families that are filled with preachers, missionaries, teachers, and church attenders. Sure, there are exceptions where God reaches down into the most ungodly situations and calls out an individual, but it appears that these are rare. The good news is that any generation can be the start of a new lineage of faithful followers. Perhaps it will begin with you!

The greatest impact upon the next generation may not be proven in the context of one's church fellowship or the safety of the home in which a person reaches maturity. Sometimes things take a turn for the worse and faith is tested far away from the roots of one's belief system.

So it was in the life of Moses.

Remember the sister of Moses. She was sent along the river bank to see what might become of little Moses as he sailed downstream from his mother's loving touch. As surely as Pharaoh's daughter was in the right place at the right time, so was Miriam. Don't forget, faith never works in isolation. Miriam's life would be directly affected by the faithful actions of her parents also. She would be able to witness firsthand the unseen guiding hand of God at work in her family's affairs.

After Pharaoh's daughter beheld the crying child, she most likely had a thought cross her mind. Who will take care of this child and feed it? Miriam, who was standing within an earshot of Pharaoh's daughter as she caressed her baby brother, heard her say, "This is one of the Hebrew children." At this moment faith was energized in this little girl. With her brother now recognized as a Hebrew male child, the danger was present that the Egyptian princess might get over her momentary compassion and throw him to the crocodiles. After all, she was the daughter of Pharaoh and her father reigned supreme in the land. But just as God had closed the mouths of the crocodiles, He opened the mouth of little Miriam. All of the faith of her parents was now transferred to a new generation and Miriam selected boldness over timidity or fear. She said to Pharaoh's daughter, "Shall I go and call a nurse for you from the Hebrew women, that she may nurse the child for you?" (Exodus 2:7)

Wow! God is good all the time! All the time, God is good!

Pharaoh's daughter tells her to go and procure a woman from the Hebrews to serve as a wet nurse for this child. Of course, Miriam did not have to search far to find just the right person. The lady she sought may have still been on her knees by the river bank. Her tears most likely were still coursing down her cheeks and dripping like raindrops on the surface of the Nile River—a river turned red by the blood of countless Hebrew babies who had died under Pharaoh's command. The lady was Jochebed, her mother and the mother of her little brother Moses.

If you think for a moment that God has no idea how much it costs to live a life of faith, you had better think again. Not only does He know how much it costs, He can make the devil pay the bill! Jochebed had built an ark out of bulrushes by faith. She had placed her baby boy inside and set him afloat amongst the crocodiles of the Nile. By faith, she waited to hear a word from her daughter Miriam of faith's selection. Through faith she received her reward! After following Miriam back to the spot of Moses' deliverance from the river, Pharaoh's daughter issues her orders, "Take this child away and nurse him for me, and I will give you your wages." (Exodus 2:9)

Double wow! God is good all the time! All the time, God is good! God is better than good—He is GREAT! Only the God of the universe could arrange for the daughter of a murderous king to rescue a child of the Hebrews, fall in love with him, give him back to his own mother for his care…

AND PAY HIS MAMA TO DO IT!

Like I said, "Ain't God good!"

Now the day came when Moses had to be given back into the care and upbringing of Pharaoh's daughter and this leads me into another round of imagination. You don't think that all Jochebed did for a couple of years was feed Moses and change diapers, do you? If so, you haven't visited my imagination!

If just half of my fancies that I have concocted about this biblical account are true, then that will be enough for me to imagine what transpired while Jochebed had Moses in her care. First, her faith must have been multiplied to new heights after her boy was delivered. Whatever she and her husband had seen in the face of Moses would now be overshadowed by God's hand of grace working in response to their faith. Indeed, this boy was destined for things beyond their wildest dreams. So Paul could say to the Ephesians with this same level of faith, "Now to Him who is able to do exceedingly abundantly above all that we ask or think, according to the power that works in us." (Ephesians 3:20)

Second, she would not have wasted a single day with Moses. She could not have known the moment that the princess would call for Moses to move into the palace. Even if she were to wait until his weaning, it was still a time that was limited. Jochebed had this moment to instill in Moses the faith that had led her to the river bank with a basket. It was her responsibility to pass this family's faith on to this child who would ultimately spend the majority of his childhood in a pagan household filled with a multiplicity of gods. She must teach him who the one true God is. She must press upon his heart and mind the songs of Zion. It had fallen to her to place under Moses the firm foundation of faith.

As Moses suckled at the breasts of his mother, I can hear her singing softly into his ear. Now I don't know what songs she would have sung then, but I can imagine what she might sing today. Her choice might be a song like:

> Come, we that love the Lord,
> And let our joys be known;
> Join in a song with sweet accord,
> And thus surround the throne.

> Let those refuse to sing,
> Who never knew our God;
> But children of the heav'nly King
> May speak their joys abroad.

The men of grace have found
Glory begun below;
Celestial fruits on earthly ground
From faith and hope may grow.

Then let our songs abound,
And every tear be dry;
We're marching through Immanuel's ground
To fairer worlds on high.

We're marching to Zion,
Beautiful, beautiful Zion;
We're marching upward to Zion,
The beautiful city of God.

As Moses would have drifted off to sleep, day after day, he would have heard the sweet prayer of his mother:

God of our fathers, the God of Abraham, Isaac, and Jacob, you know our despair in this land of Egypt wherein we are held as slaves. You are a mighty God who rewards the faithful, not because they have faith of themselves, but because you have given faith by measure to all who believe that you exist.

Oh God, hear the prayer of your servant. I offer to you this child that you not only gave to me once, but twice by faith. His life was spared on purpose. Let it now be filled with purpose.

You alone have numbered our days. You alone know the hour that is soon coming when this little child shall no longer be mine to caress. He must on that day be offered up by faith once again to live his formative years in a pagan world. But you are greater that all the gods of Egypt. You alone are the One God we serve. Let this child know this truth by faith.

Protect his eyes, his ears, his mind, and most of all his heart for the day will come when he must by faith select the course he will take. Oh, mighty King, claim him now as yours. Hold him fast to your breast as he leaves mine and when the time of choosing arrives help him by faith to make the right selection.

Forget us not in our misery as we dwell in a foreign land. If it be your will, send a deliverer!

No one knows whether Jochebed could have dreamed that she held the deliverer in her arms, but that matters not. Though we cannot know the outcome for our own children, we must never waste a single moment with them. They have been given to us for His purpose—until it is time to give them back. Until then, pray over them with the diligence of Jochebed. Never give up! Maybe you are holding a great deliverer!

And now we skip ahead to see the results of Jochebed's prayer. "By faith Moses, when he became of age, refused to be called the son of Pharaoh's daughter, choosing rather to suffer affliction with the people of God than to enjoy the passing pleasures of sin, esteeming the reproach of Christ greater riches than the treasures in Egypt; for he looked to the reward." (Hebrews 11:24-26)

All of us look for a day like this. A chance to see the fruits of faith come into full maturity. An opportunity to realize the reward of countless hours of prayer and fasting. A day of faith's selection revealed.

There is a time of selection in every person's life—a moment of decision based on faith. Moses' parents decided to place him in a basket of reeds and deposit him in the river. Moses must have heard this story from his mother countless times in those early days of his life. And now , he must make a faith decision. He decided to refuse the benefits of royalty and align himself with his people.

Another greater than Moses would be the Great Deliverer of mankind. Jesus would forsake the banner of heaven to wear a crown of thorns. Jochebed, Moses, and Jesus all made a choice based on faith. All pleased God because of it.

When Jesus was baptized a voice came from heaven saying, "This is My beloved Son, in whom I am well pleased." (Matthew 3:17) When we finish this journey called life, if it has been lived in faith, we shall hear, "Well done, good and faithful servant; you have been faithful over a few things, I will make you ruler over many things. Enter into the joy of your lord." (Matthew 25:23)

Moses forsook the pleasures of sin in the palace to take a place among his brothers in slavery. Flesh always makes decisions based upon the present; faith makes its decisions with eternity in mind.

Each of us is a product of our upbringing. We have been influenced by our home life and society as well. But, we cannot use any of this as an excuse. Moses was placed in a basket and floated down a river without his opinion. He spent the next 40 years in a pagan system without an option. Yet, when it came time to make a selection, he never paused to reflect on his past. Like the testimony of the Apostle Paul, he would have said something similar, "Brethren, I do not count myself to have apprehended; but one thing I do, forgetting those things which are behind and reaching forward to those things which are ahead, I press toward the goal for the prize of the upward call of God in Christ Jesus." (Philippians 3:13-14)

All of those precious prayers and songs of his mother came rushing back right where he was. And, by faith...

God's speaking—right where you are.

FAITH'S EMBLEM

Hebrews 11 begins with a very clear definition of faith. It is the substance of things not seen and the evidence of things hoped for in what might otherwise be hopeless and dark situations. Hopefully, (no pun intended) you have come to an understandable agreement with this definition. Now I will ask you to define faith in your life. Go ahead...take your time...okay, times up!

Hard isn't it?

When we are pressed upon to give an explanation of faith in our own lives, it sometimes gets a little fuzzy around the edges. It's like the professor who asked his students to define air in a tangible way. Each student had to present their "definition" of air before the class the next day. Many ingenious demonstrations were unfolded before the class and the professor. None were inherently incorrect, but none impressed the professor. Finally, a young lady approached the front of the classroom with nothing in hand. With no props, machines, or sleight-of-hand tricks she put her own face very near that of the professor and simply exhaled. The professor rose to his feet with a hearty, "Bravo! Well done!" This student had defined air in such a way that the professor felt the definition upon his own skin. That's what faith's emblem is all about.

An emblem is an object or its representation, symbolizing a quality, state, class of persons, etc. It is a symbol of something else. When you see an emblem, all that is behind that emblem immediately comes to the forefront.

For example, our national flag. All of us have a sense of freedom and the cost that has been paid to keep that emblem flying high. We rise to our feet; anthems are evoked; unity of mind and purpose supersede all race, creed, or religion. A simple piece of cloth bearing three colors, thirteen stripes, and fifty stars causes all of this fervor of emotion and patriotism.

So what is the emblem of faith? What stands out to define faith in such a way that you can feel it upon your skin? What stirs your heart to the degree that you are provoked to meet a challenge or change a world?

The emblem of faith is reproach. If there is one thing that proves the reality of faith to ourselves and others, it is reproach. To suffer reproach means to be defamed, abused, and taunted. The original word in the Greek comes from a word which means to receive bitter words as if being hit in the mouth by them. We use phrases to describe reproach such as: A Slap in the Face; Get Your Teeth Knocked Out; That's Too Hard To Swallow. In trying to defend the effects of reproach we say, "Sticks and stones will break my bones, but words will never hurt me!" That sounds good, but it seldom works. Words of reproach do hurt...deeply!

Why would anyone choose a path that leads to reproach? There can be only one reason: God speaks—I obey. Moses made a choice based upon the working of faith in his life. When he became of age (Hebrews 11:24) he refused to be called the son of Pharaoh's daughter. This is more than some chronological age that he attained. Moses reached a point of spiritual maturity when the work of faith was finished in his life and faith required an emblematic response. There needed to be an alignment of faith as a symbol with faith as a tangible.

It's like the illustration of our flag above. The flag is a symbol of our freedom, but it only takes on intrinsic value when the actions it has provoked are taken into account. We know that men and women have died to preserve the freedom that is only symbolically revealed in the flag. It is their actions that align the symbol of freedom with the tangible reality of the freedoms that we experience every day.

Moses made a distinct choice to align himself with the people of God as represented in the Hebrew slaves. This realignment forced him to count the cost of rejecting the treasures of Egypt and determining that the reward of God was better by "esteeming the reproach of Christ greater riches than the treasures in Egypt; for he looked to the reward." (Hebrews 11:26)

Moses became the emblem of Hebrews 11:6. Through his life we can see the reality of what happens when faith is released to do its perfect work. That step of faith pleases God and God then rewards that one who has diligently sought Him. For Moses, the consequence of making this choice was reproach. Not some everyday slap in the face. Nor was it a kick in the teeth. Reproach was not brought on by his own arrogance or disdain. His choice of reproach placed him squarely in the camp of Christ. For Moses, his troubles all began the day he made this choice.

It is not much different for you and I. As long as we are going in the same direction with the crowd, we have little if any difficulty. It is when we decide to repent and turn around that all of the resistance comes. But, oh, the happiness that can be ours upon this monumental decision. "If you are reproached for the name of Christ, blessed are you, for the Spirit of glory and of God rests upon you." (1 Peter 4:14)

Moses as faith's emblem helps us to understand how we can make the decisions that are sometimes hard. When we are called upon to respond in faith it seems that the whole world is shaped by that moment in time. The difficulty becomes a snapshot that we carry around in our pocket to remind us of just how much we had to give up because of faith. We paste it in our photo album and stick a copy on our refrigerator door for all to see. But, if we would be honest, this is just one little piece of life.

The word emblem comes from the Latin word *emblēma*. It means to be inlaid as a piece included in a mosaic. Whatever reproach you are experiencing at this moment is only a small piece of God's entire work in your life. I wrote a devotional book entitled, *Life Is Not A Snapshot: It's A Mosaic*. The title for this book did not come by accident. It came from the time I spent caring for my wife as she suffered the hardships and ultimate death brought on by Lou Gehrig's disease. I had to face each day by faith, believing that it was just one small piece of the mosaic: the emblem of faith as a whole.

Now I see faith in a whole new light. One that could have never been experienced apart from that terrible disease. My wife has already been able to exchange the reproach of Lou Gehrig's for the treasures of heaven. God has not seen fit for me to do so yet. He's still working on me! He's still inlaying one little emblematic piece of faith at a time. One day I too will leave Egypt just like Moses did. I'll get to the Promised Land. I think I've figured out what I'm going to say when I get there. It will be something like this:

"Oh, now I understand!"

Laid out before my eyes to see—for faith will no longer be necessary—will be the mosaic of my life. All of the little pieces that loomed so large as I lived them will be lost in the tapestry of His grace. Like Moses, I will be looking upon the reward. Vance Havner said of Moses, "He saw the imperishable; He saw the invisible; He did the impossible." May the emblem of our lives be so!

Billy Graham tells the following story in his devotional, *Unto the Hills.* It will help you see the work that God is doing in your life as He makes you into an emblem of faith.

During the Great Depression, a good man lost his job, exhausted his savings, and forfeited his home. His grief was multiplied by the sudden death of his precious wife. The only thing he had left was his faith, and it was weakening.

One day he was combing the neighborhood looking for work. He stopped to watch some men who were doing the stonework on a church building. One of those men was skillfully chiseling a triangular piece of rock. Not seeing a spot where it would fit, he asked, "Where are you going to put that?" The man pointed toward the top of the building and said, "See that little opening up there near the spire? That's where it goes. I'm shaping it down here so it will fit up there."

Tears filled this good man's eyes as he walked away. God had spoken to him through those words: "Shaping it down here so it will fit up there." He found new meaning in his difficult situation.

God's speaking—He's shaping your life by His words.

FAITH'S SEPARATION

We have lost an important quality of Christianity in the last few years. Some of it is simply left behind because of our lackadaisical attitude. Other parts have been lost on purpose with the idea that we can successfully co-mingle with the world and still hold our distinctiveness as Christians. I am speaking of separation.

Jesus charged the church at Ephesus of leaving their first love. "Nevertheless I have this against you, that you have left your first love. Remember therefore from where you have fallen; repent and do the first works, or else I will come to you quickly and remove your lampstand from its place—unless you repent. (Revelation 2:4-5) This church did not lose their love; it was misplaced. They were doing a lot of good things and leaving behind the best.

I can hear the detractors howling that I would include the idea of the church living out faith in such a way that we separate ourselves from the world. "How will we reach the lost, the unchurched, or the newly designated underserved people of the world?" they ask with great passion. I know that you mean well, but I cannot get past the fact that when Moses' faith was energized, he left Egypt. "By faith he forsook Egypt, not fearing the wrath of the king; for he endured as seeing Him who is invisible." (Hebrews 11:27)

He did not flee Egypt out of fear; he forsook Egypt because he saw "Him who was invisible." The best way to see the visible is by seeing the invisible. This can only be done by faith. Faith required a distinct separation from all that he had known before as the son of Pharaoh's daughter.

Understandably, this separation will not preach well in the 21st century, but does that make it any less a valid truth? A.W. Tozer commenting on Ephesians 4:31 said, "As Christian believers, we must stand together against some things. So, if you hear anyone saying that A.W. Tozer preaches a good deal that is negative, just smile and agree: 'That is because he preaches the Bible!'

Here are some of the things we oppose: we are against the many modern idols that have been allowed to creep into the churches; we are against the 'unauthorized fire' that is being offered on the altars of the Lord; we are against the modern gods that are being adopted in our sanctuaries.

We are against the world's ways and its false values. We are against the world's follies and its vain pleasures. We are against this world's greed and sinful ambitions. We are against this world's vices and its carnal habits."

The world he is describing sure sounds a lot like Egypt to me! How about you?

Well, you say, can't we still mix a little with the world? Isn't it possible just to visit Egypt and then scurry back to God's side of the tracks? Jesus not only spoke to the Ephesians about leaving their first love, He spoke to the Laodecians about their lukewarmness. "These things says the Amen, the Faithful and True Witness, the Beginning of the creation of God: I know your works, that you are neither cold nor hot. I could wish you were cold or hot. So then, because you are lukewarm, and neither cold nor hot, I will vomit you out of My mouth." (Revelation 3:14-16)

The last time I checked there are still two faucets on most sinks: one for hot water and one for cold water. There is no lukewarm faucet. If you want lukewarm water, you will have to mix portions of hot water and cold water. The result is from co-mingling and Jesus says that it matters to the point that He vomits it out of His mouth.

The cost for Moses was great. He left everything behind in Egypt. Relationships and riches were left in the shadow of the pyramids. He made the decision to risk everything by faith. His parents had taken the risk of placing him in a basket and setting him afloat in the crocodile infested Nile River. He took the risk of siding with the Hebrew people and turning his back on the easy life of the palace. He did all of this by keeping his eye fixed on that which is invisible so he could partake of the imperishable and accomplish the impossible.

A faith that risks nothing quickly degenerates into a religion of mediocrity. We will always seek the path of least resistance and thereby miss the blessings of God's hand at work.

His decision led him away from the security of Egypt to the solitude of the sand dunes on the backside of the desert. But it was in this sequestered isolation that he experienced God speaking from the burning bush. Who wouldn't want to have such an experience? All of us surely would, but it will never happen in Egypt! Burning bushes are for the separated—those who have risked all by faith.

The Apostle John understood this for he wrote, "By this we know that we love the children of God, when we love God and keep His commandments. For this is the love of God, that we keep His commandments. And His commandments are not burdensome. For whatever is born of God overcomes the world. And this is the victory that has overcome the world—our faith." (1 John 5:2-4) Certainly this is how John could withstand the isolation of exile upon the

Isle of Patmos. It was here that God spoke to John and we have the final book of the Bible, the book of Revelation.

God's speaking—somewhere out of Egypt.

FAITH'S MEANS

If you haven't figured it out by now, the means by which faith is set in motion is through obedience. Nothing discussed thus far nor anything that will be included hereafter is possible apart from obedience. God speaks—I obey. If you get that ingredient of your Christian life in order then everything else will fall into place.

Hebrews 11:28 follows 40 years of Moses living on the backside of the desert. Seemingly out of nowhere God speaks. "Now Moses was tending the flock of Jethro his father-in-law, the priest of Midian. And he led the flock to the back of the desert, and came to Horeb, the mountain of God. And the Angel of the LORD appeared to him in a flame of fire from the midst of a bush. So he looked, and behold, the bush was burning with fire, but the bush was not consumed. Then Moses said, 'I will now turn aside and see this great sight, why the bush does not burn.' So when the LORD saw that he turned aside to look, God called to him from the midst of the bush and said, 'Moses, Moses!'" (Exodus 3:1-4)

From this encounter God instructs Moses to return to Egypt and deliver the children of Israel. This should be good news to those who have had a problem with the previous section of this chapter. Though separation is needed if we are going to hear from God, it may lead us back to rescue others still trapped in Egypt.

Faith brings us out in order to bring us in. Obedience takes us to the place of training and development, then it can protect us as we live out the promises of God.

Moses returned to Egypt, but it was not with good news for the Egyptians. After a series of plagues that wreaked havoc upon the Egyptians, a final blow from the hand of God was delivered. For the Israelites it would henceforth be call the Passover. For the Egyptians it would be remembered as The Night of Death. Hebrews 11:28 records this event. "By faith he kept the Passover and the sprinkling of blood, lest he who destroyed the firstborn should touch them."

God promised the Israelites that the last plague would not harm them. They only needed to kill a spotless lamb then place its blood on the doorposts and lintel of the house where they lived. This last plague would pass them by. The life of their firstborn would be saved. It was a night of faith lived out to the max.

There may have been one of four responses to this command of God concerning a sacrificial lamb being slain and the blood applied to the doorways of the Israelite homes. Though the scripture does not state these responses by the Israelites, I think that they can be assumed by the responses of people in our day to the redeeming work of Christ upon the cross.

Why bring the cross into this last plague that was about to fall upon Egypt? The picture of the cross can be easily seen if you follow the commands of God concerning the night of the Passover. These instructions are recorded for us in Exodus 12.

Each household was to take a lamb on the tenth day of the month and bring it into the home. On the fourteenth of that month the lamb was to be killed. Exodus 12:7 instructs them to, "take some of the blood and put it on the two doorposts and on the lintel of the houses where they eat it." Following these instructions the lamb would be slain at the door. Using a branch of hyssop dipped in the lamb's blood, a marking of blood would be made on the two doorposts and on the lintel (the overhead crossbar that finishes the frame) of the door. Do you see in this the four points of the cross? The lamb was slain where the feet of Jesus would have been on the cross. The door posts would each represent the position of his hands as they were nailed to the horizontal beam of the cross. The blood on the lintel would mark the place where he hung his beaten brow now pierced by the thorns of a cruel crown.

This picture of the cross, clearly seen in the actions of the Israelites on the night of the Passover, is despised by many, ignored by others, and gladly received by believers. Imagine with me the following scenes that relate both to the night of the Passover and to the Cross of Jesus Christ.

When Moses told the people what God had commanded, I'm sure there were some that simply rejected the whole concept. After all, who did Moses think he was? Missing for 40 years on the back side of some desert certainly left him in a bad light in the opinion of some. These people would have missed the opportunity of their firstborn being spared because of their obstinacy. When God passed throughout the land on the fourteenth night of the month, the firstborn in these households died. They died even though they were Israelite! No one is saved by heritage. Everyone is saved by the blood.

Another response may have been like many today who simply don't like the idea of a bloody religion. These would have procured a lamb on the tenth of the month. By the fourteenth they would have fallen in love with the lamb and they just could not bring themselves to kill it as prescribed by God's command. They would have tied it at the door that night. With the lamb bleating away at the door, the march of death would have come and their firstborn would have died. Many are like these families. They love Jesus, but they just cannot fathom that He would have to die for their sins. A firm grasp of religion is in their hands. Prayers are lifted up to doors of brass and bounce back unanswered. Their cry is heard in the night as their substitute for a sacrifice fails to keep death outside the door.

The third group is very common. They believe what God has said about selecting a perfect lamb on the tenth of the month. The lamb is slain as required on the fourteenth day. They consume the lamb as required. "Then they shall eat the flesh on that night; roasted in fire, with unleavened bread and with bitter herbs they shall eat it." (Exodus 12:8) They are dressed just as the command of God had required. "And thus you shall eat it: with a belt on your waist, your sandals on your feet, and your staff in your hand. So you shall eat it in haste. It is the LORD's Passover. (Exodus 12:11)

But...they do it all with fear and trembling! The joy of obedience is not theirs. The family is religiously correct in all they do, but there is no hallelujah said when they find their firstborn safe in his bed. How many today serve God this way? Out of duty and demand the orders are fulfilled and the blessedness of following Him is lost. Isaiah tells us in his prophecy that there is supposed to be peace in connection to the following of God's command. "Oh, that you had heeded My commandments! Then your peace would have been like a river, and your righteousness like the waves of the sea."

(Isaiah 48:17) Jesus responding to an unnamed woman from one of the crowds that followed Him said, "More than that, blessed are those who hear the word of God and keep it!" (Luke 11:28) The word blessed in this verse means happy. There should have been an anticipation filled with the bliss of assured promise, but this family missed it.

Saved, yes. Happy, no. How often do you find yourself trudging through religious activity? Are you confident of heaven someday, but missing the hilarious joy of serving Jesus with the promise of His purpose making all things work together for your good (Romans 8:28)?

Finally, we come to the fourth response that was surely seen on this ghastly night in Egypt when the firstborn of so many homes died. Imagine a family sitting in their humble abode. Hard, indeed, to call it a house since it belongs to slaves. Roasting on the fire is the body of the little lamb that had given its life at the door just a few hours earlier. The scent of unleavened bread wafts its way into each corner of the house. The pungent smell of bitter herbs adds accent to the moment. Each family member is fully dressed with sandals tied. Father has his staff in hand. The hour draws nigh when God shall fulfill His promise and set the captives free.

Prayer is offered before a hastily consumed meal is enjoyed by all. Smiling faces are noted on each—especially upon the face of the firstborn son. His life is guaranteed. His salvation is secure. Neither by his own hand, but by the life of a little lamb. This lamb paid a price he did not owe for a debt no one in the house could pay.

All over Egypt the wail slowly rises through the night air. One home after another experiences the judging hand of God. Firstborn after firstborn die needlessly. All that was needed had been provided, yet refused. The condemned could have lived, but decided not to yield to the word of God. Grace could have been theirs, but instead judgment.

All is now lost as louder and louder the cries are heard, but not in this house. The little family holds their firstborn tightly and listens to his every breath. Mother feels the beating heart of her son against her breast. The family shall never forget this night. This moment shall forevermore be marked in their minds. Like that moment that you first heard the good news of the gospel and yielded your life to the Lamb who had given his life for you. That place emblazoned upon your heart will be revered as holy.

Now with a gift from my imagination, I give them a song to sing in the night. A song that would not in fullness be realized for nearly 2000 years. A song that would follow the words of John the Baptist, "Behold! The Lamb of God who takes away the sin of the world!" (John 1:29) Will you not sing it with them now?

> I hear the Savior say,
> "Thy strength indeed is small;
> Child of weakness, watch and pray,
> Find in Me thine all in all."
>
> For nothing good have I
> Whereby Thy grace to claim;
> I'll wash my garments white
> In the blood of Calv'ry's Lamb.
>
> And now complete in Him,
> My robe, His righteousness,
> Close sheltered 'neath His side,
> I am divinely blest.

Lord, now indeed I find
Thy pow'r, and Thine alone,
Can change the leper's spots
And melt the heart of stone.

When from my dying bed
My ransomed soul shall rise,
"Jesus died my soul to save,"
Shall rend the vaulted skies.

And when before the throne
I stand in Him complete,
I'll lay my trophies down,
All down at Jesus' feet.

Refrain:
Jesus paid it all,
All to Him I owe;
Sin had left a crimson stain,
He washed it white as snow.

~Elvina M. Hall, 1865~

Dear friend, let not one of these first three responses be yours. If you have rejected the Lamb of God, receive Him today! Has yours been a life of callous religious regard for Jesus? Accept Him slain to set you free from religion's chains. Do you spend each day worried if the price has been enough? Should more have been done to secure your salvation? Could more have been done? Trust that these questions are answered in the words of Jesus from the Cross, "It is finished!" (John 19:30)

God's speaking—rejoice in His finished work.

R.E. Clark

FAITH'S BOLDNESS

We may not always think about being bold in our faith, but, there is no doubt that one of the boldest moves that could be made by Moses was to cross the Red Sea. Actually, scripture tells us that it was God that led the children of Israel to the shore of the Red Sea. "Now the LORD spoke to Moses, saying: 'Speak to the children of Israel, that they turn and camp before Pi Hahiroth, between Migdol and the sea, opposite Baal Zephon; you shall camp before it by the sea...'" (Exodus 14:1-2) God Himself placed millions of Hebrews in a predicament where only a bold faith would suffice. There was no room for a weak or indecisive faith.

I have already written about this entire episode in the first book of this series. *God's Leading: 7 Ways To Know God Is Leading You* will fill you in on all of the reasons I believe God directed Moses to lead the people to this particular spot on the beach. With the Egyptian army closing in from behind and an impassable body of water before them, nothing short of a bold move of faith would bring about the miracle needed.

Many seem to be happy with their deliverance from sin's penalty and even more happy to rest just outside the city limits of Egypt. God's plan is for us to move on to the Promised Land and the way there will take us through some places that require an extreme faith. As Paul penned his letter to the Philippians from a Roman prison he said, "But I want you to know, brethren, that the things which happened to me have actually turned out for the furtherance of the gospel, so that it has become evident to the whole palace guard, and to all the rest, that my chains are in Christ; and most of the brethren in the Lord, having become confident by my chains, are much more bold to speak the word without fear." (Philippians 1:12-14)

The word translated as bold in these verses comes from a Greek word that means to be venturesome and courageous through extreme conduct. Paul concludes that his brothers in Christ are being boldly faithful because of his predicament. Here again, you can see the similarity of both Paul's and Moses' situations. In both cases, God led them into these situations. With Paul, others spoke the word boldly without fear. With Moses, God declared that the people were to move forward even with the sea before them (Exodus 14:15).

Faith brings us out of Egypt to bring us through the trials that lie in our path. Even something as large as the Red Sea can be changed into dry ground by a bold faith. We have no reason to fear what man can do when we are moving ahead in the boldness of faith. William Secker, a seventeenth-century clergyman, in speaking about the boldness of the believer said, "Another singular action of a sanctified Christian is to prefer the duty he owes to God to the danger he fears from man. Christians in all ages have prized their services above their safety. 'The wicked flee when no man pursueth: but the righteous are bold as a lion.' The fearful hare trembles at every cry; but the courageous lion is unmoved by the greatest clamors. Were believers to shrink back at every contrary wind that blows, they would never make their voyage to heaven." Oh, that we might see men and women of faith proceed through the days of their Christian lives with such bold faith!

This Moses standing on the shore of the Red Sea was the same Moses that had stood before the burning bush. At the first encounter he offered excuses to God as to why he could not possibly act as Israel's deliverer. Standing before several million people, who stared at the impossibility of crossing the water that lay before them, Moses lifted his hand over the sea and watched it turn into dry land (Exodus 14:21).

Moses had been delivered from the waters of the Nile as a baby. Now he was delivered through the waters of the Red Sea. His faith life began in the water and was proven in the water. The faith of his mother had expanded from the deliverance of one little baby to the safe passage of a multitude.

The boldness of faith opened a highway for the Israelites and built a graveyard for the Egyptians. Hebrews 11:29 tells us that the Egyptian army attempted to use the dry sea bed to chase down the children of God. They thought they could take by force the miracle of God. They did not know what you and I know: "But without faith it is impossible to please Him, for he who comes to God must believe that He is, and that He is a rewarder of those who diligently seek Him." (Hebrews 11:6)

God's speaking—be bold in your faith

FAITH'S VICTORY

Everyone loves a winner. Parades are for victors, not losers. This holds true in sports, politics, beauty pageants, etc. Name it and we will celebrate with the winners every time. Losers crawl away into the sunset never to be heard from again.

Don't be discouraged by this opening paragraph. Here's the good news: God doesn't spend any of His time surveying the win loss columns. He is not enamored by the latest political guru that has burst upon the scene. As for beauty, none can compare to that held by a lily of the valley.

When you consider Israel's victory over the city of Jericho, it must be taken in a broader context. How about a 40 year context? When Jericho was conquered it was Israel's second chance at getting this Promised Land thing right. Hebrews 11:30 places the fall of Jericho next to the fall of the Egyptian army under the waters of the Red Sea. "By faith they passed through the Red Sea as by dry land, whereas the Egyptians, attempting to do so, were drowned. By faith the walls of Jericho fell down after they were encircled for seven days." (Hebrews 11:29-30)

A look back at the history of Israel's conquest of the Promised Land shows a less than stellar performance. But this is where faith comes into play. Without faith nothing is either pleasing to God or possible without Him. When the two words "by faith" are added to the equation, walls fall down flat. Here's what happened 40 years earlier.

God commanded Moses to choose twelve men, one from each tribe of Israel, to go and spy out the land of Canaan. The men were to "'see what the land is like: whether the people who dwell in it are strong or weak, few or many; whether the land they dwell in is good or bad; whether the cities they inhabit are like camps or strongholds; whether the land is rich or poor; and whether there are forests there or not. Be of good courage. And bring some of the fruit of the land.' Now the time was the season of the first ripe grapes." (Numbers 13:18-20) These spies were not going of their own accord. They were under the command of God Himself. Theirs was only to obey. God even made it easy! Moses told them to bring back some of the fruit of the land and they just "happened" to be going at the season of the first ripe grapes! Sure sounds like a done deal—NOT!

The men made the incursion without incident. They returned after 40 days with a sampling of the fruit and reports of a land flowing with milk and honey. It should have been a victory, but it was not. Where faith ended, failure followed.

Only Joshua and Caleb gave a report based on faith. The majority brought a negative report to the people. With faith out of the picture, these men turned their eyes from faith's evidence and began to see with their physical eyes only. "Then they told him, and said: 'We went to the land where you sent us. It truly flows with milk and honey, and this is its fruit. Nevertheless the people who dwell in the land are strong; the cities are fortified and very large; moreover we saw the descendants of Anak there. The Amalekites dwell in the land of the South; the Hittites, the Jebusites, and the Amorites dwell in the mountains; and the Canaanites dwell by the sea and along the banks of the Jordan. There we saw the giants (the descendants of Anak came from the giants); and we were like grasshoppers in our own sight, and so we were in their sight.'" (Numbers 13:27-29; 33)

Like I said earlier, "Everyone loves a winner," but this day was not one of the best in Israel's history. They refused to believe God by faith and it cost them one year of wandering in the wilderness for every day they had been in the land of Canaan. Don't ever think that the choice of living without faith comes with no expense to you. Before Israel was given another chance to believe God and act in faith, all of the men above the age of 20 had died. Thousands of funerals were held each day in the wilderness, because a negative report of faithlessness had been given by the perceived majority. What Israel had forgotten was that God is always a majority all by Himself. God never loses! It doesn't matter what the scoreboard of life reads at any given moment.

One of my favorite illustrations is about a man watching little league baseball. He had stationed himself near the outfield and was watching a little fellow as he "played". The boy's glove lay on the grass while he squatted down to pick as many four-leaf clovers as he could find.

The man called to the boy, "Who's winning?"

The little baseball player spoke without looking up, "They are."

"What's the score?" inquired the onlooker.

Again, without any distraction from his search for clovers, he replied, "It's 22 to nothing."

Uncertain if he should ask, the man's curiosity got the best of him. "Who's winning?"

"They are," said the outfielder with no particular sound of despair in his voice.

"Aren't you sad or discouraged at the score?" said the man.

"Nope!" retorted the boy. "We ain't been up to bat yet!"

Now that's what I call the victory of faith! Something tells me that boy's name just might be Joshua or Caleb. He wasn't looking at the scoreboard any more than Joshua and Caleb were measuring or counting giants.

Caleb quieted the crowd after the majority report had been given. "Let us go up at once and take possession, for we are well able to overcome it." (Numbers 13:30) The group of ten faithless men thought they would be eaten like grasshoppers by the giants. Joshua declared otherwise: "The land we passed through to spy out is an exceedingly good land. If the LORD delights in us, then He will bring us into this land and give it to us, 'a land which flows with milk and honey.' Only do not rebel against the LORD, nor fear the people of the land, for they are our bread; their protection has departed from them, and the LORD is with us. Do not fear them." (Numbers 14:7-9) Makes you wonder what barbequed giant tastes like, doesn't it?

Two simple truths come from the story of Jericho's destruction. First, faith requires no effort on our part. Second, faith requires every effort on our part. These two statements do not conflict with each other, instead, they complement each other.

After 40 years of wilderness wandering, Israel now stands on the brink of victory. Before them stands a formidable obstacle as seen in the walled city of Jericho. The removal of this obstacle was beyond the capability of the Israelites. Impossibility does not fit into the faith equation, because with God all things are possible (Matthew 19:26). God speaks to Joshua with the good news of victory even before the battle was engaged. "And the LORD said to Joshua: 'See! I have given Jericho into your hand, its king, and the mighty men of valor.'" (Joshua 6:2)

Faith requires no effort on our part because God has already given the victory. But, faith requires every effort on our part, for the next statement of God to Joshua includes all of Israel in the victory party. "'You shall march around the city, all you men of war; you shall go all around the city once. This you shall do six days. And seven priests shall bear seven trumpets of rams' horns before the ark. But the seventh day you shall march around the city seven times, and the priests shall blow the trumpets. It shall come to pass, when they make a long blast with the ram's horn, and when you hear the sound of the trumpet, that all the people shall shout with a great shout; then the wall of the city will fall down flat. And the people shall go up every man straight before him.'" (Joshua 6:3-5)

This is exactly how Paul reduces this miraculous act on God's part and the complete obedience of His people in Hebrews 11:30. The walls came down by faith in the word of God. God said it—that settles it! Could God have simply reduced the walls of Jericho to rubble? Yes, of course, He could have, but He chose to include His people in the process. The exact instructions were given with the intent on God's part that they be obeyed. When done so, victory happens!

John concluded the same thing as he wrote, "For whatever is born of God overcomes the world. And this is the victory that has overcome the world—our faith." (1 John 5:4)

God's speaking—Obey and the victory is yours!

Mileposts

Why was it a particularly difficult time for Moses to be born?

_____
_____
_____
_____

How did the faith of Moses' parents save his life? How did God reward his mother for her work of faith?

_____
_____
_____
_____

What is the emblem of faith? Can we rejoice when we see this emblem in our lives? Why?

_____
_____
_____
_____

In what ways did Israel act in faith to bring down the walls of Jericho?

_____
_____
_____
_____

Fill in the blanks:

A _____ that _____ nothing quickly degenerates into a _____ of _____.

Chapter Five

THE SURPASSING OF FAITH

So far we have discussed the substance of faith, the sending of faith, the sacrifice of faith, and the surrender of faith. Paul had laid forth the principle of faith (Hebrews 11:1-22), then the practice of faith (Hebrews 11:23-30), and now lists for us some personalities of faith that might seem unlikely candidates (Hebrews 11:30-32). He concludes Hebrews 11 with the product of faith.

FAITH'S SALVATION

One of the strongest proofs when it comes to believing in the inspiration of the Bible is the characters that God has included. If the Bible was only written as a compilation of people's lives that we could follow by example, then somebody must have made a mistake!

One after another you can add men and women to your list that simply were not the best examples of humanity. Liars, cheaters, adulterers, murderers, and prostitutes are all included. Their lives are laid open and bare for our examination. This one attribute of the scripture alone is full proof for me that the Bible is indeed the inspired and infallible word of God. No mere man in his right mind would have included any of these people in the narrative.

And that brings us to Rahab—the harlot. As Rahab is introduced in the list of the faithful, Paul assumes that you and I know her story. He simply states, "By faith the harlot Rahab did not perish with those who did not believe, when she had received the spies with peace." (Hebrews 11:31) Everyone may not be familiar with her story, so we will need to once again visit the Old Testament account. Here, we will see how she came to this place of faith in her life and ultimately how she and her household were saved on the day the walls fell down at Jericho.

In Joshua 2, the story unfolds of how two spies were sent into Canaan while the children of Israel were encamped on the other side of the Jordan River. These men infiltrated the walls of Jericho and were taken under the protective care of Rahab. After it had been discovered that these spies were in the land, she was questioned of their whereabouts. She hid the men and later slipped them out her window to safety.

Her introduction in Hebrews 11 tells us that she was functioning by faith, but where did this faith come from and upon whom did it rest? Again, the book of Joshua fills in the details for us. Here is her testimony.

"I know that the LORD has given you the land, that the terror of you has fallen on us, and that all the inhabitants of the land are fainthearted because of you. For we have heard how the LORD dried up the water of the Red Sea for you when you came out of Egypt, and what you did to the two kings of the Amorites who were on the other side of the

Jordan, Sihon and Og, whom you utterly destroyed. And as soon as we heard these things, our hearts melted; neither did there remain any more courage in anyone because of you, for the LORD your God, He is God in heaven above and on earth beneath." (Joshua 2:9-11)

Did you notice where she begins her testimony? She begins not with Israel just across the Jordan River. Her words are not based on current events, but upon events that had occurred 40 years before! The people of Jericho had become fearful four decades earlier when news had reached them of the dividing of the Red Sea. The spies may have seen giants in the land on their first approach, but their faithlessness forced them to turn around and spend 40 years wandering in the wilderness. All of this time, the inhabitants of Canaan were quaking in their sandals!

I'm afraid that you and I miss many a blessing because we do not understand the powerful impact that faith has upon the world around us. Like ripples flowing out from that little basket that Moses' mother placed in the Nile so many years before, the wake of faith had now rolled its way all the way to Jericho. Israel could have ridden that wake all the way to victory, but they saw the height of the giants instead.

How many times have you taken your eyes off of Jesus and slipped beneath the waves of doubt? Circumstance is always trumped by faith! When we choose to live a life of faith, it not only affects our day but it also affects life for generations to come.

Rahab declared that the hearts of the people in Jericho had melted to the point that no courage was left. But then, she adds her statement of faith. Up to this point she was simply stating the facts, but now she responds in faith. This is why Hebrews tells us that by faith she did not perish.

"...for the LORD your God, He is God in heaven above and on earth beneath. Now therefore, I beg you, swear to me by the LORD, since I have shown you kindness, that you also will show kindness to my father's house, and give me a true token, and spare my father, my mother, my brothers, my sisters, and all that they have, and deliver our lives from death."(Joshua 2:11-13)

Her fear was translated into faith even as scripture tells us, "The fear of the LORD is the beginning of knowledge, but fools despise wisdom and instruction."(Proverbs 1:7) Rahab was saved by faith. She did not attain this faith of her own accord. This verse from Proverbs tells us that fools despise wisdom and instruction. Without the fear of the Lord, we remain fools. The term means one that is incapable of attaining knowledge.

Rahab's condition as she addressed the spies was exactly the same as it is for every person on planet Earth: lost in her foolishness and in need of the gift of faith. But here is the good news. "For by grace you have been saved through faith, and that not of yourselves; it is the gift of God, not of works, lest anyone should boast." (Ephesians 2:8-9) By the time the spies had arrived in her home, God had already been there delivering the gift of faith to her heart. Rahab was not saved by her faith in the Hebrew spies, but in the God of the Hebrew spies. You cannot be saved by faith in another person or through another person's faith. Faith in God alone is the only remedy for being lost without Christ. Faith in God alone saved Rahab. Faith in God alone can save you too!

The spies instructed her to act upon her faith by identifying her home as the one where they had hidden. "So the men said to her: 'We will be blameless of this oath of yours which you have made us swear, unless, when we come into the land, you bind this line of scarlet cord in the window through which you let us down, and unless you bring your father, your mother, your brothers, and all your father's household to your own home."' (Joshua 2:17-18) A scarlet cord hanging from her window would protect her from the coming invasion. Not only would she be saved from destruction, but all of her family she could gather in her home would be safe as well.

The Scarlet Thread

For years she heard the stories told
The mighty acts of One unknown,
Of seas made dry and kings now gone,
Would all the horrors now unfold?

A knock upon her door one day
Two Hebrew spies lay low,
Knowing not the way to go,
Protect would she or give them both away?

Hidden well among her stuff
Jericho sought them in her home,
She sent them far away to roam
Would she now these spies rebuff?

By faith the truth revealed
Openly made known her fear,
"Spare my family and I," said she with a tear
Would you give your oath as a shield?

A scarlet thread hang in your window
The spies confidently spoke in grace,
Behind this blood red cord, our God embrace
Safe shall you be and safely shall you go.

If you ever conclude that the effort to bring your family to Christ is being wasted, think again. Bring them in; explain the meaning of a scarlet cord hanging in the window of your heart; and watch God bring the evidence of amazing grace to your family.

Rahab was saved out of a city filled with unbelievers. She experienced the gift of faith; and God, in all of His ways that are beyond our understanding, included her in the lineage of Christ. It all began by faith. It will always continue by faith. For this reason Jesus could pray in John 17, "I do not pray that You should take them out of the world, but that You should keep them from the evil one. They are not of the world, just as I am not of the world. Sanctify them by Your truth. Your word is truth." (John 17:15-17) He has us here in all of our imperfections, like a harlot named Rahab, to demonstrate to the world how incredible the work of faith is in the human life. And maybe...just maybe, we might get to hide a family member or friend behind a scarlet cord of faith.

God's speaking—He speaks
through the most unlikely persons.

FAITH'S SUFFICIENCY

'Nuf said!

There comes a time when enough has been said on any given subject. This is NOT one of those times. Neither was it for the Apostle Paul. He begins this final portion of what we know as Hebrews 11 by saying, "And what more shall I say?" (Hebrews 11:32) He then goes on to say a lot. Paul was my kind of preacher! Beware when a preacher says, "Finally..." It doesn't really mean much!

Paul begins with this verse a long sentence in the original language. It continues all the way through Hebrews 11:38. His list of the faithful continues as he mentions three judges and the commanding general of another judge from Israel's history. "And what more shall I say? For the time would fail me to tell of Gideon and Barak and Samson and Jephthah…" (Hebrews 11:32)

We should be able to relate well to this period of Israel's history since it so much parallels our own day. This time was noted as a time in which everyone was doing that which seemed right in their own eyes (Judges 21:25). The entire book of Judges is the story of Israel's backsliding into idolatry and God then sending a rescuer. These judges would deliver them from the oppressors that had overtaken them in their time of rebellion. God would bless once again and then they would falter in their walk with God. Faithfulness and the lack thereof are the constant themes of the book.

Yet out of this troubled time rises four men whose names are recorded here in Hebrews 11. Once again, God uses unlikely characters to demonstrate how faith at work needs little to work with in a presentation of God's glory. Each of these judges were used by God in spite of their deficiencies.

Gideon appeared on the scene at a time of oppression by the Midianites. He was actually hiding in a winepress threshing wheat when the Angel of the Lord appeared to him with words that did not match the character of the man. This was another pre-Bethlehem incarnation of Jesus Christ. This same Angel of the Lord had wrestled with Jacob and shown Himself as the Commander of the Lord's host to Joshua. To Gideon he proclaims, "The LORD is with you, you mighty man of valor!" (Judges 6:12)

The response of Gideon was far from being one of faith. "Gideon said to Him, "O my lord, if the LORD is with us, why then has all this happened to us? And where are all His miracles which our fathers told us about, saying, 'Did not the LORD bring us up from Egypt?' But now the LORD has forsaken us and delivered us into the hands of the Midianites." (Judges 6:13) It gets worse, however!

After the Angel of the Lord declares that Gideon will be the deliverer of Israel (Judges 6:16), Gideon asks for a series of signs to prove the call upon his life. The first is given to Gideon when the Angel touches the meal that has been prepared and it is consumed by fire (Judges 6:21). This might be an acceptable request on Gideon's part though it still lacked faith on his part. He wanted to be sure that it was really God who was speaking.

You would assume that such a demonstration would convince the biggest skeptic, but Gideon was still weak in his faith. After hearing a second time from God, he obeys in the destroying of the altar of Baal. Judges 6:27 informs us that he is still operating out of fear instead of faith because he takes ten additional men with him to do the job. He also uses the cover of nightfall to complete the task for fear of his own father's household.

A turning point for Gideon occurs when the Spirit of the Lord comes upon him (Judges 6:34) and he calls out the fighting forces to confront the Midianites and the Amalekites in the Valley of Jezreel. Years later God would say through the prophet Zechariah, "So he answered and said to me: This is the word of the LORD to Zerubbabel: 'Not by might nor by power, but by My Spirit,' says the LORD of hosts." (Zechariah 4:6) Surely, after the Spirit of God falls upon Gideon he would be ready to face anything…but not so. He still lacked faith enough to obey God.

We respond likewise many times when God calls upon us to do a task that is beyond ourselves. Maybe this is why we only ask God for tasks that we can accomplish in our own strength. Instead, we should be asking God to make us equal to the task at hand. Only when we attempt that which is beyond our own strength will God get all of the glory. It will only be in these times that we respond in faith and thereby please Him.

Gideon uses two additional tests to prove that which God had already spoken clearly to him. He even states the fact that he had already heard God's speaking: "If You will save Israel by my hand *as You have said...*" (Judges 6:36, emphasis mine). These two tests are what many affectionately call laying a fleece before the Lord. We have justified our own lack of faith by glamorizing Gideon's actions. We have assumed that because God yielded to his request concerning the fleece (Judges 6:37-40) that it is perfectly fine for us to test God in the same way.

This story of the fleece serves to prove the frailty of Gideon's faith, but it in no wise gives us a prescription for finding out God's will. God had already spoken—that should have settled it. For some reason God took these extra steps to prepare Gideon for taking on the oppressors. It does not serve as a model for you and I to follow when we already have clear evidence of God's speaking.

I am grateful that God helps us in our time of unfaithfulness, but we should never rely on wet or dry fleece to prove God's will. Ask Him to help you always seek the filling of His Spirit and a measure of faith that will equal whatever the task is at hand. The amazing part of this entire story is that God saw fit to list Gideon in Hebrews 11 as an example of faithfulness. It sure leaves us with little excuse!

Gideon was filled with fright instead of faith, but in the end God used him to bring glory to Himself. When Gideon shows up with 32,000 fighters, God goes about the process of paring them down to only 300. It is just a little funny that Gideon loses 22,000 after he proclaims, "'Whoever is fearful and afraid, let him turn and depart at once from Mount Gilead.' And twenty-two thousand of the people returned, and ten thousand remained." (Judges 7:3) What could he say? He started out himself hiding in a winepress and going during the dark to destroy the altar of Baal.

I can only imagine that he must have gotten very nervous when 22,000 men walked away from the fight. God, however, doesn't use the same math as you and I when odds are being calculated. "But the LORD said to Gideon, 'The people are still too many; bring them down to the water, and I will test them for you there. Then it will be, that of whom I say to you, 'This one shall go with you,' the same shall go with you; and of whomever I say to you, 'This one shall not go with you,' the same shall not go.'" (Judges 7:4)

When it comes time to determine what resources you need, always let faith enter into the calculations. In my book, *God's Leading: 7 Ways to Know God Is Leading You*, I use the following analogy: I am nothing; just a big zero. God is the only One that matters. If you take a great big zero and put a One in front of it you get **10**. Take two of us zeros and put a One in front and you get **100**. Do you see where this is going? **1000; 10,000; 100,000; 1,000,000...** Now image God as a One in front of 301 zeros! It really didn't matter what number of troops Gideon ended up with after God was finished. It only mattered that God was in the front of all the zeroes!

This is how faith works in our lives. It's getting God out front and us following Him wherever He leads. When

Gideon and his 300 men marched down the hillside blowing trumpets while breaking clay pitchers with torches inside of them, it certainly didn't look like a well thought out plan. How could 301 overcome an unnumbered host? Simple! You just let God go first! And that's exactly what Gideon did. Listen to his words, "When I blow the trumpet, I and all who are with me, then you also blow the trumpets on every side of the whole camp, and say, 'The sword of the LORD and of Gideon!'" (Judges 7:18)

There is the order of faith when faith becomes all sufficient in our lives. It was the sword of the Lord going first and then the sword of Gideon. It took Gideon a while to get there, but he finally responded to the circumstances in faith. He let God go first and followed Him with his zero strength. Because of this, God was pleased to give the victory!

God's speaking—Get ready for the victory!

Fear kept Gideon from living out his faith in the beginning of his career as a judge of Israel, but Paul gives us three others as examples. The second of these was Barak. Barak's deficiency was his hesitancy. Could faith be found to be sufficient in light of this?

One of the amazing things about grace is that God can overcome all of our fallacies and intricacies. Someone has said it well this way:

God Does Not Call The Qualified
He Qualifies The Called

Barak served under the judgeship of Deborah, the only female judge to rule in Israel. Israel had once again slipped into apostasy and God placed them under His chastising hand. Jabin, a king of Canaan, and his commander Sisera had oppressed the people for 20 years when the children of Israel began to cry out to the Lord for deliverance (Judges 4:1-3).

Deborah called for Barak to assemble 10,000 men and make them ready for battle. The time had come for Israel's deliverance once again. But Barak was hesitant. It is evident that he had already delayed in preparing for battle (Judges 4:6), but it gets worse. He decides to hide behind a woman's skirt tail.

Now before you ladies who are reading this get angry, this has nothing to do with women's rights or men's wrongs. It has everything to do with being obedient to God's command. Deborah was right in her chastisement of Barak. God had ordained her to serve as judge. He had given her the mission to destroy Sisera and told her how to accomplish it. It was only Barak's duty to perform as she had directed. He did not...he hesitated.

Finally he said to Deborah, "If you will go with me, then I will go; but if you will not go with me, I will not go!" I have heard all sorts of explanations for his actions, but none of them resolve the issue for me. Some have suggested he wanted her to go out of honor for her role as judge or some other tradition common to the day. Deborah, however, did not see it this way. Her response was frank and to the point. "So she said, 'I will surely go with you; nevertheless there will be no glory for you in the journey you are taking, for the LORD will sell Sisera into the hand of a woman.' Then Deborah arose and went with Barak to Kedesh." (Judges 4:9)

I must be honest here. I find great difficulty in finding faith in the story of Barak. But he is listed in Hebrews 11 by the inspiration of the Holy Spirit. Therefore, he was faithful beyond what we might see of him in the book of Judges.

If there is one bright spot it must be in this statement by Deborah as the battle was about to ensue. "Then Deborah said to Barak, 'Up! For this is the day in which the LORD has delivered Sisera into your hand. *Has not the LORD gone out before you?*' So Barak went down from Mount Tabor with ten thousand men following him. And the LORD routed Sisera and all his chariots and all his army with the edge of the sword before Barak; and Sisera alighted from his chariot and fled away on foot." (Judges 4:14-15, emphasis mine)

I think that it was at this point that the faith of Barak was released unto the work. Deborah told Barak that the Lord had gone before him. It was then that Barak engaged the battle and pursued the enemy until all were destroyed.

Once again we see the same story unfold. Barak, a zero, could only be faithful after God, the One, went out in front of Him. Like Gideon shouting, "The sword of the Lord and of Gideon," Barak lost his hesitancy when he was told that God was out front.

There was, however, a cost for his hesitancy. Deborah has told him that because of his insistence that she go with him to battle, God would give the final blow to a woman instead of him. As Sisera fled the battle he went into the tent of Jael and there she killed the commanding general of the king of Canaan.

When God's speaking—never hesitate!

Faith is truly sufficient even in the midst of our own insufficiencies. The same God who created all that is out of nothing (remember Hebrews 11:3) is the same God who can make faith evident in those who have nothing to offer. Gideon was frightful while Barak was hesitant. Can it get any more messy than this? Isn't faith hard enough to explain without God listing these men in the hall of faith? It does get worse when we consider the life of Samson.

Paul now includes Samson in his list of the faithful. When the life of Samson is examined it begins well, falters in the middle, and thankfully ends as it had begun—though with great cost.

Samson was a miracle child. Like Isaac was to Abraham and Sarah, so Samson was to his parents. He was a promised child to a childless couple. His mother, Manoah, received a heavenly visitor who proclaimed that she would bear a son. (Judges 13:7) Here again a pre-Bethlehem incarnation of Jesus is seen. He is called A Man of God in this verse. Furthermore, a special instruction is given to Manoah that her son should be set aside under a Nazarite vow from the womb to his death. Samson was to never drink wine, eat a special diet, and never cut his hair as a Nazarite. He would become a judge to deliver Israel once again. This time from the Philistines.

With this background, one would assume a wonderful outcome to faith's workings, but it was not to be. Samson, like many of us, started out well, but fell to another fleshly trait: flippancy. Flippancy is defined as unbecoming levity or pertness especially in respect to grave or sacred matters. Samson could not control his own passions. The wisest man who ever lived, Solomon, said in one of his Proverbs, "Whoever has no rule over his own spirit is like a city broken down, without walls." (Proverbs 25:28)

His wild passions led him to marry pagan women and his anger took him on wild pursuits of revenge. Yet through all of this, time and again, the Spirit of the Lord would come upon him allowing him to accomplish mighty acts (Judges 14:19). Faith proves itself to be a gift over and over in these lives. It leaves you and I without excuse in our faithful service to Him who reigns on high.

Samson's greatest failure was in his relationship with Delilah (Judges 16). Using her charm and deceit, she convinces him to reveal the secret of his strength: "... he told her all his heart, and said to her, 'No razor has ever come upon my head, for I have been a Nazirite to God from my mother's womb. If I am shaven, then my strength will leave me, and I shall become weak, and be like any other man." (Judges 16:17)

The mistake that Samson made in his faith life is very similar to that made by many today. We begin to take a flippant attitude toward the things of God. We somehow think that faith exists because of some internal quality present in our lives. For Samson, he concluded that it was his hair. He, like us, forgot that the secret to his strength lay outside of himself. Our strength is resourced in the presence of God's Spirit in our lives. Judges 16:20 tells the horrible outcome of forgetting this truth: "But he did not know that the LORD had departed from him."

Because of his departure from faith, he was taken captive by those whom he had been called to judge. His eyesight was destroyed as the Philistines gouged out his eyes; he was bound by strong cords; and he was forced to serve as a grinder in the prison. All of this because of a flippant attitude toward faith.

Blinded, he was forced to walk by faith. Without his freedom, he was forced to find liberty in God's truth. Under heavy labor, he leaned on the everlasting arms and found rest. In time, he discovered that our God is a God of second chances. Faith despised can be revived! So it was in Samson's life. So it can be in your life.

In the end, Samson slew more Philistines in his final day of living than he had in all of his life. "So it happened, when their hearts were merry, that they said, 'Call for Samson, that he may perform for us.' So they called for Samson from the prison, and he performed for them. And they stationed him between the pillars. Then Samson said to the lad who held him by the hand, 'Let me feel the pillars which support the temple, so that I can lean on them.'

Now the temple was full of men and women. All the lords of the Philistines were there—about three thousand men and women on the roof watching while Samson performed. Then Samson called to the LORD, saying, 'O Lord GOD, remember me, I pray! Strengthen me, I pray, just this once, O God, that I may with one blow take vengeance on the Philistines for my two eyes!' And Samson took hold of the two middle pillars which supported the temple, and he braced himself against them, one on his right and the other on his left. Then Samson said, 'Let me die with the Philistines!' And he pushed with all his might, and the temple fell on the lords and all the people who were in it. So the dead that he killed at his death were more than he had killed in his life." (Judges 16:25-30)

God's speaking—It's time to return!

So Paul has given us three men whose lives are less than stellar examples of faith—at least not as men measure faithfulness. Gideon was frightful. Barak was hesitant. Samson was flippant. Sound like anyone you know? Surely, this is enough of humanity in all of its weakness for us to get the point! Evidently not. Paul adds another of the judges to his list just so we will get the full picture. He now introduces us to a little known judge by the name of Jephthah.

I would not suspect that you have heard a message preached lately on the life of Jephthah. His story is tucked away in two chapters of the book of Judges. His was a life of stark contrast. He is introduced is an unusual way. "Now Jephthah the Gileadite was a mighty man of valor, but he was the son of a harlot; and Gilead begot Jephthah. Gilead's wife bore sons; and when his wife's sons grew up, they drove Jephthah out, and said to him, 'You shall have no inheritance in our father's house, for you are the son of another woman.'" (Judges 11:1-2)

Jephthah is noted as a mighty man of valor that came from a very tough background. Born out of harlotry, he was rejected by his half-brothers and driven away from his home. He becomes what might be known today as a gang leader (Judges 11:3). Sure sounds like the making of a man of faith!

Well, actually you would think not. Jephthah would fall under the category of undesirable in many churches today. He would be one of "those bus kids" that tear up the church and cost us more than he's worth. Yes, he may not sound like a man of faith, but this is the very kind of fellow that God can use to bring Himself glory.

By and by, trouble came to the land as the Ammonites declared war against Israel. Who do you think everyone thought of as a deliverer? You got it…Jephthah! One thing about a man of troubles, he knows how to deal with trouble.

God wastes nothing in a person's life. All of the hardships that Jephthah had experienced growing up would now be used as a source of strength in his life to serve as a judge over Israel. Are there things in your life that you hesitate to look back upon today? Have you long ago counted incidents in your life as wasted moments or unrecoverable broken relationships? Don't take God out of the equation!

Remember, He works all things together for good according to His purpose (Romans 8:28).

Jephthah stands mightily against the Ammonites and contends for Israel from a position of strength based upon the promised provision of God. Once again scripture attests to the fact that without God we can do nothing. "Then the Spirit of the LORD came upon Jephthah, and he passed through Gilead and Manasseh, and passed through Mizpah of Gilead; and from Mizpah of Gilead he advanced toward the people of Ammon." (Judges 11:29)

If the story of Jephthah's life ended at this point it would make it a lot easier to fit him into Paul's list of the faithful. But he is in the list and his life doesn't end with a military victory to his credit. Just like our lives, things sometimes get messy...or at the least they get hard. Not only do they get hard, but they are made difficult by our own decisions.

I have noted the most glaring deficiencies in the other men who were included in Paul's list: fear, hesitancy, and flippancy. If I were to attribute one word to describe Jephthah it would be rash.

Jephthah acted in a most impulsive manner. Perhaps his hastiness came from his childhood. He was looked down upon by his half-brothers and he would have certainly had to struggle in each situation that confronted him. Living among and fighting alongside ruffians probably developed an attitude of "you snooze, you lose." At any rate, Jephthah's weakness in this one area cost him dearly. It cost him the life of his daughter.

"And Jephthah made a vow to the LORD, and said, 'If You will indeed deliver the people of Ammon into my hands, then it will be that whatever comes out of the doors of my house to meet me, when I return in peace from the people of Ammon, shall surely be the LORD's, and I will offer it up as a burnt offering.'" (Judges 11:30-31)

On the surface, Jephthah's vow seems harmless and sincere. He is demonstrating his faith in God to deliver Ammon in his hands and he is desirous to proclaim his allegiance and reliance unto the Lord in making such a vow. Certainly, he could have never imagined the outcome. He most likely would have imagined some animal running out to meet him upon his return, but it was not to be.

"When Jephthah came to his house at Mizpah, there was his daughter, coming out to meet him with timbrels and dancing; and she was his only child. Besides her he had neither son nor daughter." (Judges 11:34) His response was like any father's response would be: "And it came to pass, when he saw her, that he tore his clothes, and said, "Alas, my daughter! You have brought me very low! You are among those who trouble me! For I have given my word to the LORD, and I cannot go back on it." (Judges 11:35)

If you have never read this account of Jephthah's vow before this day, then you may be aghast at the thought of a father sacrificing his daughter. I have read it many times and I still find myself with deep-seated and mixed emotions. We just cannot imagine such a scenario. But, here it is for our consideration. Not only is it recorded in biblical history, it confronts us in the hall of faith.

Once more the proof of inspiration is made evident by Jephthah's inclusion in Paul's list of faithful men. It would have been easier to just ignore him, but the Spirit of God moved the pen of Paul to record him alongside the others. So, what do we do with him? How do we explain his actions?

Quite simply, we don't do anything with him. His life is recorded for our instruction. "For whatever things were written before were written for our learning, that we through the patience and comfort of the Scriptures might have hope. Now may the God of patience and comfort grant you to be like-minded toward one another, according to Christ Jesus, that you may with one mind and one mouth glorify the God and Father of our Lord Jesus Christ." (Romans 15:4-6) Jephthah's life is there to bring us hope and that ultimately we might glorify God as always being right in all He does.

As far as explaining Jephthah's actions, I don't try to do so. Others might attempt explanation. Some might contrive unique cultural dynamics that would somehow allow his daughter to escape. Many would proclaim that God would never allow Jephthah to sacrifice his daughter in light of His prohibition against such. I will not do so. I will only take the word at its face value and conclude that I cannot explain everything.

In the end, whether Jephthah's daughter was sacrificed or somehow set aside unto the Lord matters not. He made a vow—he kept his vow—and that was a supreme act of faith on his part. It was so much so that Paul includes him here in Hebrews 11 with men like Gideon, Barak, and Samson. He is included because we all have made rash statements in our lives that cost us dearly in the end. The question is not if we will do so, but when. Then we must ask, "Will I follow through in faith to do as I have so promised before the Lord?"

God's speaking—sometimes we can't explain it.

Paul now leaves the lives of the judges and concludes his list of faithful personalities with a king and a prophet. As in each of the previously discussed lives, faith was needed to surpass the deficiency of human life. So far we have seen that faith can overcome fear, hesitancy, flippancy, and rashness. Now Paul lists as an example of faith none other than King David, a man noted as one who was after God's own heart. "…He raised up for them David as king, to whom also He gave testimony and said, 'I have found David the son of Jesse, a man after My own heart, who will do all My will.'" (Acts 13:22)

It does not take us long to see that David lived a life of faith. Being chosen as an unlikely successor to the throne of Israel, noted as a slayer of giants, and suffering as a man who lived months on the run from a king gone mad, all served to form a life of faith in David. If any of the men listed in Hebrews 11:32 deserved to be there it was David, right? Well, hold on to your horses!

Paul inserted David right in the midst of these faithful characters who each had their own set of shortcomings. It makes no sense to conclude that David would be the odd man out in Paul's logic. He is there because he too needed the surpassing of faith. He needed a faith that would work beyond his own deficiencies.

David was not a man of fear. He had slain the lion and the bear with his bare hands. He was not hesitant like Barak when it came to battle. He was not flippant like Samson for he was always aware when he sensed a need for the renewing of God's Spirit. "Create in me a clean heart, O God, and renew a steadfast spirit within me. Do not cast me away from Your presence, and do not take Your Holy Spirit from me. Restore to me the joy of Your salvation, and uphold me by Your generous Spirit." (Psalm 51:10-12)

He was not a man of rash decisions. He had more than one opportunity to forcefully remove Saul from the throne, but he refused to lay his hand upon God's anointed. Instead, he chose to wait upon God to act in righteousness. What then was David's weakness? What caused Paul to place this great king of Israel in the list of faith at this particular place?

David needed the surpassing of faith in his life to overcome his own sensuous nature. Perhaps Paul placed David's name here in the list because some who would read his letter might conclude by this time that they were above all of the idiosyncrasies of the characters he had included. All who would read David's name, however, would remember also the name of Bathsheba.

The story of David and Bathsheba unfolds like the sordid details of a modern day soap opera. David had overcome a multiplicity of difficulties in his ascension to the throne of Israel. His life up to this point reveals faith in its finest hour.

Yet, like so many who have followed after him, the day came when he let down his guard. When David's faith was not exercised it resulted in a forsaking of his values. "It happened in the spring of the year, at the time when kings go out to battle, that David sent Joab and his servants with him, and all Israel; and they destroyed the people of Ammon and besieged Rabbah. But David remained at Jerusalem. Then it happened one evening that David arose from his bed and walked on the roof of the king's house. And from the roof he saw a woman bathing, and the woman was very beautiful to behold." (2 Samuel 11:1-2)

David's faithless response to seeing Bathsheba bathing sends out ripples that affect her, her husband, the child that is born of this relationship, and eventually all of Israel. Just as faith sends out ripples to affect generations to come, so do unfaithful acts as well.

David conceives a plan to have Uriah, the husband of Bathsheba, killed. The child of David and Bathsheba dies in infancy. Israel is affected by the wars that follow as the legacy of David's rule as king. "Now therefore, the sword shall never depart from your house, because you have despised Me, and have taken the wife of Uriah the Hittite to be your wife." (2 Samuel 12:10)

David's sensuousness was a very real weakness in his life, but David should be included here in faith's hall of fame. More than any of the others listed in Hebrews 11, we see faith's surpassing in his life. His faithfulness is noted over and again throughout his life. It is easy to see the man of faith as he pens so many of the Psalms. There is none that reflects his dependency in faith upon his God more than Psalm 23:

> The LORD is my shepherd; I shall not want.
> He makes me to lie down in green pastures;
> He leads me beside the still waters.
> He restores my soul;
> He leads me in the paths of righteousness
> For His name's sake.
> Yea, though I walk
> through the valley of the shadow of death,
> I will fear no evil;
> For You are with me;
> Your rod and Your staff, they comfort me.
> You prepare a table before me
> in the presence of my enemies;
> You anoint my head with oil;
> My cup runs over.
> Surely goodness and mercy shall follow me
> All the days of my life;
> And I will dwell in the house of the LORD
> Forever.

David's weaknesses were surpassed by faith. He could always know the way because he followed the Shepherd in faith. His shortcomings were resolved by faith. He rested through faith. He was restored by faith. He faced death and all manner of evil by faith. He was protected in faith. He was blessed through faith. He saw a city not made with men's hands by faith. As God spoke in David's life, he was always ready to hear.

God's speaking—follow Him!

Paul brings us to the end of the named characters of faith as he includes one of the prophets: Samuel. Here is a life begun in the miracle of faith as seen in his mother's prayer for a child. Here is a man of faith who early in life had to learn how to hear God speaking. Here is a man of faith who was on the scene as Israel became a monarchy. And like all of the others, here was a man who had his own moments of faithlessness.

Samuel's story, like that of Moses, begins in his mother's faith. His mother Hannah was barren and sought the Lord year by year for a child to be borne by her. She suffered greatly under the ridicule of her husband's second wife who had borne children unto him. With the brokenness of her heart overflowing she made a vow unto the Lord. "Then she made a vow and said, 'O LORD of hosts, if You will indeed look on the affliction of Your maidservant and remember me, and not forget Your maidservant, but will give Your maidservant a male child, then I will give him to the LORD all the days of his life, and no razor shall come upon his head.'" (1 Samuel 1:11)

God answered the prayer of Hannah which she had asked in faith and unto her was born in due time a son. She named him Samuel. Even Samuel's name made reference to the faith that had brought him into the world. "So it came to pass in the process of time that Hannah conceived and bore a son, and called his name Samuel, saying, 'Because I have asked for him from the LORD.'" (1 Samuel 1:20)

Hannah's vow did not go unfulfilled. As Jephthah had kept his vow, so Hannah kept hers. The day came when little Samuel was weaned from his mother's breasts and she went up to offer him in continual service before the Lord at Shiloh (1 Samuel 1:24). In both of these cases, Jephthah and Hannah refused the temptation to not keep their vows. Both of these people exhibited great depths of faith in their actions. They knew the commitment that was required upon making a vow before the Lord. The wisest man who ever lived would say years later: "When you make a vow to God, do not delay to pay it; for He has no pleasure in fools. Pay what you have vowed—better not to vow than to vow and not pay. (Ecclesiastes 5:4-5)

When you take the time to unpack the lives behind these men and women of Hebrews 11, you begin to see that all of them had lives that were similar in so many ways. Imagine Hannah's life as a new mother for a moment. Each day would shine with thankfulness unto God for His answer to her prayer. She would hold Samuel with a dearness that was based not upon her having her son next to her for years to come, but knowing that the day would soon come that her vow would need to be fulfilled.

Her life was no different than the life of Moses' mother. She, too, had a limited time to hold and caress her little boy. Like Moses, who was released to the palace of Pharaoh, Samuel would need to be released to the care of Eli in the house of the Lord at Shiloh. Hannah would have spent these days as Jochebed had spent hers. Each day would have been filled with the instruction of a lifetime. Over and again, she would have whispered her love into his ear. Each night she would have tucked him into his crib, knowing that one less day was now hers to hold him as her own. Hannah at least knew that Samuel was on his way to the Lord's house. In this she could be comforted.

As a side note, you might like to know that God always honors those who by faith honor Him. Hannah gave Samuel to the Lord as she had vowed. She returned to her home "childless." Would God let this act of faith go unrewarded? Would she once again fall under the ridicule of others? Would some declare her to be a foolish woman for living this standard of faith? Remember, Hebrews 11:6 gives us this promise, "But without faith it is impossible to please Him, for he who comes to God must believe that He is, and that He is a *rewarder* of those who diligently seek Him. (emphasis mine)" Indeed, God did reward Hannah's faith. "And the LORD visited Hannah, so that she conceived and bore three sons and two daughters. Meanwhile the child Samuel grew before the LORD." (1 Samuel 2:21)

Once again the ripples of faith have reached out to touch another life. Spanning the years and many lives, faith now is demonstrated in the life of Samuel. We do not know how old Samuel was when he was lent to the Lord (1 Samuel 1:28). We do not know how old he was when he was awakened in the night by the voice of God. First Samuel 3:1 calls him a boy which can mean any age from infancy to adolescence. The important thing here is not how old Samuel was, but that the word of the Lord was heard. It was a rare thing in those days. "Now the boy Samuel ministered to the LORD before Eli. And the word of the LORD was rare in those days; there was no widespread revelation." (1 Samuel 3:1) It is a rare thing in our day as well!

Three times God called out to Samuel. Each time Samuel would run to Eli, the priest, thinking that it was he who was calling for him (1 Samuel 3:4-8). The amazing thing here is not that Samuel was ignorant of God's voice, but that it took Eli three times to become aware of what was happening. Years later a prophet would arise in the stead of Samuel and declare, "My people are destroyed for lack of knowledge. Because you have rejected knowledge, I also will reject you from being priest for Me; because you have forgotten the law of your God, I also will forget your children." (Hosea 4:6) Oh, that we might respond in faith to the voice of God!

Samuel's life served as a bridge from the time of the judges to the time of the kings. God used Samuel as both judge and prophet. He would guide the people of Israel through the choosing of their first king, Saul. He presided over the anointing of Saul's replacement, David. When he died all of Israel lamented his passing (1 Samuel 25:1).

How does Samuel fit in with Gideon, Barak, Samson, Jephthah, and David? Why did Paul include him by name in this list of faithful personalities? Was there a need for faith's surpassing in Samuel's life as well? He certainly was not fearful, for he stood before King Saul and rebuked his faithless actions (1 Samuel 15). He was not hesitant, as demonstrated by his quick response to God calling his name. He was not flippant concerning his call, as noted by all of Israel lamenting his death after many years of faithful service. He was not rash in his decisions, as seen in him seeking out a replacement for King Saul (1 Samuel 16:11). There is no indication of a sensuous life. Scripture does not even record the name of his wife. We can assume that he had only one, but we do know that he had two sons.

It is at this point that Samuel can be added to this list as found in Hebrews 11:32. Samuel needed the surpassing of faith because he was careless.

It was not with his ministry, for all of that seemed well cared for in its entirety. Samuel, like so many, did well with his public ministry, but failed with his own family. Carelessness led his own two sons to act more like the sons of Eli than his own. "Now it came to pass when Samuel was old that he made his sons judges over Israel. The name of his firstborn was Joel, and the name of his second, Abijah; they were judges in Beersheba. But his sons did not walk in his ways; they turned aside after dishonest gain, took bribes, and perverted justice." (1 Samuel 8:1-3)

In this one area of his life he failed to watch carefully and it cost him dearly. His sons did not walk in his ways...the ripple of faith that had passed over him as a child failed to reach his own children. How can this happen?

It very seldom happens on purpose. Few fathers would make the decision to put obstacles in the path of their children's spiritual development. It happens most often by an almost imperceptible drift. Hebrews 2:1 states it well: "Therefore we must give the more earnest heed to the things we have heard, lest we drift away." The idea here is of a boat that is loosely tied to the pier and with the rising tide becomes disconnected to its mooring. With one lap of the water after another, the boat is carried away in the current.

The scripture tells us that Samuel was old when he appointed his sons to be judges, but they had drifted from their father's faith. They no longer fulfilled the demands of their position. Herein, Samuel's carelessness led Israel to demand a king instead of his sons' rule as judges. Again, we see the ripple effect of faith and/or faithlessness at work.

We all need to take heed lest we drift away. The lives of these six men have been laid bare for our consideration. We need not make the same mistakes that they made, but chances are very high that we will fail in our faith life at some point.

We will need to look back and see that it is not *their* faith that preserved them, but *God's* faithfulness!

"If we confess our sins, He is faithful and just to forgive us our sins and to cleanse us from all unrighteousness." (1 John 1:9)

"...being confident of this very thing, that He who has begun a good work in you will complete it until the day of Jesus Christ." (Philippians 1:6)

"If we are faithless, He remains faithful; He cannot deny Himself." (2 Timothy 2:13)

"Let us hold fast the confession of our hope without wavering, for He who promised is faithful." (Hebrews 10:23)

God's speaking—be faithful to hear.

Let me remind you once again that Hebrews 11:32-38 is one very long sentence in the original Greek translation. This is important to remember because the six men whose lives we have just unfolded for you are connected to all that follows in the next six verses. Paul will summarize all the rest of the history of faith in this short space. These six personalities of faith lay the foundation by their actions for all of the product of faith.

James said with certainty that faith without works is dead. "Thus also faith by itself, if it does not have works, is dead." (James 1:17) Paul follows this same line of thought by adding a compilation of accomplishments to the faith of those hitherto listed.

It was through faith that these men and women were able to subdue kingdoms. You and I may not be going on a conquest anytime soon, but there are indeed kingdoms that need to be overturned by faith. Paul told the Corinthians, "For though we walk in the flesh, we do not war according to the flesh. For the weapons of our warfare are not carnal but mighty in God for pulling down strongholds, casting down arguments and every high thing that exalts itself against the knowledge of God, bringing every thought into captivity to the obedience of Christ..." (2 Corinthians 10:3-5) We fight these battles of mind and soul each day. These struggles of the flesh can all be won by faith.

By faith we can do the right thing in every situation. You know that there always seems to be many options available when it comes to making decisions. But there will always be only one right decision. This concept of working righteousness means to act according to character that is based upon justification. We do not make decisions based upon our own sense of right and wrong, but upon God's character. We function as one who has been made right in His sight. When we make right choices as Christians, we always know that we do so only because He has at some point in time made us righteous. So with Abraham, "He did not waver at the promise of God through unbelief, but was strengthened in faith, giving glory to God, and being fully convinced that what He had promised He was also able to perform. And therefore 'it was accounted to him for righteousness.'" (Romans 4:20-22)

The work of faith is made effectual in the promise of God. These all obtained the promise of God. This is no mere recognition of the promise; it is a seizing upon and holding dear. *A* promise becomes *the* promise when it becomes *my* promise. In his book, *Daily Gems*, Dwight L. Moody commented about the breath-taking beauty of the Alps. He said that houses of faraway villages can be seen with great distinctness, so that sometimes the number of panes of glass in a window can be counted. The distance looks so short that the place to which the traveler is journeying appears almost at hand. This is because of the clearness of the atmosphere. We sometimes dwell in high altitudes of grace, and Heaven seems very near…At other times the cloud and fog caused by suffering and sin cut off our sight. However, we are as near Heaven in the one case as we are in the other, and we are just as sure of gaining it.

So it is with the promises of God. We claim them by faith—not by sight. And even when they seem beyond our belief we will not stagger, knowing that God will never fail to keep His word.

Paul now recounts the product of faith in a very tangible fashion. Through faith the mouths of lions are closed, fires are quenched, the sword is escaped, weaknesses are overcome, battles are won, and even death is mastered. Persecutions cannot withstand the full impact of faith. Torture is tempered. Ridicule by false accusation cannot result in a repudiation of faith. Physical abuse nor prison can break faith's hold upon one's life. All manner of abuse is without its intended result. Homelessness only creates a greater desire for a city made without hands.

Now you and I may not have to suffer very much if any of these trials and persecutions in our lifetimes, but there is a world outside of our borders that faces it daily. We are much more likely to face the mouth of a gossip rather than the mouth of a lion. The fire of lust and desire is more likely to burn us than an actual death at the stake. It might be the sword of judgmental attitudes that cut us before our necks are exposed to the blade. Yet in all of these ways we will need faith at its best so that we might be overcomers of all.

More often than not, faith is demonstrated in our lives by endurance rather than deliverance. We will need to join with the Apostle Paul in declaring, "Therefore I take pleasure in infirmities, in reproaches, in needs, in persecutions, in distresses, for Christ's sake. For when I am weak, then I am strong. (2 Corinthians 12:10)

A missionary who had experienced many heartbreaking episodes in his life was asked how he could be so cheerful. His response tells the story of faith and that which it produces in its maturity. He replied, "If someone sent me on a journey and warned me that I would come first to a dangerous river crossing, then to a forest filled with wild beasts before I had reached my destination, I could only endure these with the assurance that as I experienced each it was proof that I was on the right road."

Jesus promised that in this life we would have much tribulation. Should we not rejoice when it comes that it is proof to us that we are walking the right road? Seek not deliverance, but endurance. For as we endure we join a long list of many faithful who have preceded us. Not only do we join them, they have for so long awaited our arrival on the scene. Paul concludes his thoughts on faith in Hebrews 11:39-40, "And all these, having obtained a good testimony through faith, did not receive the promise, God having provided something better for us, that they should not be made perfect apart from us."

Somehow in God's economy none of these faithful could be declared complete in their faith without us who are alive right now at this very moment. The ripples of faith are still moving outward and have now encompassed your life. Your response to the voice of God will complete the faith of men and women like Abel, Enoch, Abraham, Sarah, Jochebed, Moses, Gideon, Samson, David, Hannah, and Samuel.

As you respond to his voice in faith, new ripples will be sent out to affect other generations that will follow. May it be that we remain faithful unto His coming! May the question Jesus asked during His earthly ministry be answered in the affirmative. "Nevertheless, when the Son of Man comes, will He really find faith on the earth?" (Luke 18:8)

God is speaking to us as surely as He spoke to all of the men and women listed in Hebrews 11. It's time to respond in faith!

God's speaking—I obey!

Mileposts

In what ways was the faith of Rahab strengthened by the history of God's dealings with Israel?

_____

_____

_____

_____

Was Gideon correct or incorrect in how he responded when God called him to deliver Israel? Why or why not?

_____

_____

_____

_____

Match each faith character to the description stated by the author.

Gideon	Rash
Barak	Frightful
Samson	Careless
Jephthah	Sensuous
David	Flippant
Samuel	Hesitant

Fill in the blanks:

The _____ of faith is made effectual in the _____ of God.

ABOUT THE AUTHOR

R.E. CLARK currently serves as an associational missionary in Arkansas. He earned his D.Min. from the Southern Baptist Center in Jacksonville, Florida. He served as a pastor in four churches before beginning his service as the associational missionary to the 70 churches, missions, and ministry points of the Northwest Baptist Association in Bentonville, Arkansas.

His writing comes from life experiences which include over 34 years in ministry. Before his call to ministry he was a business owner. His devotional life deepened and his writing career began in 2008 after the death of his wife Kay from Lou Gehrig's Disease. He has written two yearlong devotional books: *Glasses in the Grass: Devotions For My Friends* and *Life Is Not A Snapshot: It's A Mosaic.*

Following his devotional writing, he began writing a four part series of Bible studies. Each of these helps the reader understand the journey of their life. The first of these Bible studies is *God's Leading: 7 Ways To Know God Is Leading You.* The second, *God's Designing: Evidences For the Christian Life*, precedes this book. The fourth in this series, *God's Giving,* will be released very soon. He has also authored a book on revival. *Expecting Revival* includes a history of revival in America, the biblical basis for revival, and a manual for forming teams that will prepare the church for a heaven-sent revival.

He has been blessed in his second marriage to Trudy. Trudy's first husband, a police officer, was killed in the line of duty. Together they have 8 children, 17 grandchildren, and one great-grandchild. They reside in Centerton, Arkansas.

Contact the author:

Email: reclark@reclarkauthor.com
Facebook: R.e. Clark
Twitter: @GlassesnGrass
Pinterest: reclarkjr
LinkedIn: R.E. Clark

www.ingramcontent.com/pod-product-compliance
Lightning Source LLC
Chambersburg PA
CBHW060927040426
42445CB00011B/829